AMERICAN EDUCATION

Its Men,

Ideas,

and

Institutions

Advisory Editor

Lawrence A. Cremin
Frederick A. P. Barnard Professor of Education
Teachers College, Columbia University

AMERICAN EDUCATION: *Its Men, Ideas, and Institutions*
presents selected works of thought and scholarship that have
long been out of print or otherwise unavailable. Inevitably, such
works will include particular ideas and doctrines that have been
outmoded or superseded by more recent research. Nevertheless,
all retain their place in the literature, having influenced educational thought and practice in their own time and having provided
the basis for subsequent scholarship.

The AMERICAN ROAD *to* CULTURE

A Social Interpretation of Education in the United States

By

GEORGE S. COUNTS

ARNO PRESS & THE NEW YORK TIMES
*New York * 1971*

Reprint Edition 1971 by Arno Press Inc.

Reprinted from a copy in
The State Historical Society of Wisconsin Library

American Education:
Its Men, Ideas, and Institutions - Series II
ISBN for complete set: 0-405-03600-0
See last pages of this volume for titles

Manufactured in the United States of America

Library of Congress Cataloging in Publication Data

Counts, George Sylvester, 1889-
    The American road to culture.
    (American education: its men, ideas, and
institutions. Series II)
    1. Education--U. S. 2. Education--Philosophy.
I. Title. II. Series.
LA210.C6 1971   370'.973   70-165736
ISBN 0-405-03605-1

The American
Road to Culture

The AMERICAN ROAD *to* CULTURE

A Social Interpretation of Education in the United States

By

GEORGE S. COUNTS

New York
THE JOHN DAY COMPANY

PRINTED IN THE U. S. A.
FOR THE JOHN DAY COMPANY, INC.
BY THE QUINN & BODEN CO., INC., RAHWAY, N. J.

To

JOHN DEWEY

ABOUT THE AUTHOR

GEORGE SYLVESTER COUNTS was born in Baldwin City, Kansas, in 1889. He was educated at Baker University and at the University of Chicago. From 1916 until 1927 he was, successively, head of the department of education at Delaware College, Newark; professor of educational sociology at Harris Teachers College, St. Louis; professor of secondary education at the University of Washington; professor of education at Yale University; and professor of education at the University of Chicago. Since 1927 Dr. Counts has been associate director of the International Institute and professor of education in Teachers College, Columbia University. He served as special investigator of education in the Philippines in 1927, and in Russia in 1927 and 1929.

Dr. Counts is the author of several previously published volumes, among them: *The Selective Character of American Secondary Education, The Senior High School Curriculum, The Social Composition of Boards of Education, Secondary Education and Industrialism, School and Society in Chicago, Principles of Education* (with J. C. Chapman), and *Education in Soviet Russia* (in *Soviet Russia in the Second Decade*). He is also editor of *The New Education in the Soviet Republic*, by A. P. Pinkevitch.

PREFACE

THE present volume represents an effort to abstract from American social and educational practice the principles and ideas that shape the conduct and evolution of education in the United States. I fully realize of course that this is an extremely hazardous undertaking and that in all probability no two persons faced with the task would perform it in the same way or arrive at the same conclusions. Personal bias and experience must inevitably enter into a work of such a character. This fact of course I have realized fully from the very first. Indeed I was so conscious of my own limitations and of the great difficulties to be surmounted that I withheld the manuscript from the press for eight months after its completion. And as I write these lines I look forward with some misgivings to the day when the volume will issue from the press.

Nevertheless, in spite of the difficulties, I am convinced that an attempt at a broad social and theoretical interpretation of American education should be made. Even if the project be not well executed, it should serve the very useful purpose of centering attention on the fact that educational theory, to be effective, must be part and parcel of a particular civilization and must sustain a most intimate relationship with social life and institutions. It should also stimulate thinking on the more fundamental educational questions faced by our society. I trust, moreover, that this effort of mine will provoke some of my colleagues in the profession to similar endeavors. If they disagree with either my analysis or my interpretation, as no doubt many of them will, I hope that they will undertake to paint the picture as they see it. And the more radical and complete their disagreement, the more spirited and fruitful should prove the discussion.

In surveying the situation I have sought to divest myself, in so far as that is possible, of any strictly American experience or point of view and examine our program of education from a relatively detached position. In fact I have endeavored to look at America through the eyes of a foreign observer. Whether I have achieved any measure of success in this attempt my readers must be the judge. My only comfort is that I have done the job as honestly as I could.

In striving for objectivity and fruitful viewpoints I feel that I have been greatly aided by the observations of numerous foreign educators who have visited the United States in recent years under the auspices of the International Institute. Sojourns in other countries have also proved very helpful in enabling me to view American education from a distance. My visits to Russia in particular, because of the radical nature of the Soviet experiment, have challenged my thinking on both educational and social questions. No one can dwell long in Moscow without realizing that he is living in *the other half of the world*. The consequence is, I think, a gain in perspective which can be secured in no other way.

In addition to foreign educators, whom I have encountered both here and abroad, I am greatly indebted to many of my American friends. Professor John Dewey has been for me, as he has been for all of his contemporaries, an inexhaustible source of inspiration and stimulation. In this undertaking I have received numerous suggestions from several of my colleagues in Teachers College: Professors W. H. Kilpatrick, J. H. Newlon, I. L. Kandel, E. H. Reisner, Harold Rugg, R. B. Raup, and Harold Clark. To Doctor Newlon I am particularly indebted because he read the entire manuscript and called my attention to a number of errors of judgment. It is perhaps unnecessary to say, however, that my friends are in no way responsible for the general conclusions to which I have come. The volume as a whole is my responsibility alone.

GEORGE S. COUNTS.

New York City
April 26, 1930

CONTENTS

The American
Road to Culture

CHAPTER I

CONTROLLING IDEAS IN AMERICAN EDUCATION

THERE are two approaches to the educational theory of any advanced country. The one is through the writings of its great educators, and the other is through the forms which its educational institutions have assumed. In most studies of educational theory the former is the approach which has been followed. Indeed the history of pedagogy, as ordinarily written, has been an account of the thought and the writings of educational theorists. Such an approach possesses the merit of dealing with materials which are entirely tangible and definite. In the systems of thought developed and elaborated by individual men educational theory, being made the object of explicit attention, is given a certain logical consistency and completeness which educational institutions commonly lack. Hence there is a natural temptation to write the educational theory of a people or of a civilization in terms of the names and the thoughts of its great educational theorists.

Another reason for the common adoption of this first approach to the study of educational theory is no doubt found in the widespread assumption that the institutions of a people flow directly and inevitably from the thought of its theorists. Certainly in the case of education in the United States such a simple view of causation can find little support. Again and again the evolution of American educational institutions has proceeded with but little regard for the pronouncements of leading educators. In fact in many instances the latter apparently have totally misread the spirit of the age and have found themselves overwhelmed and borne along on the stream of events by social forces which they neither sensed nor understood. The thought of philosophers is often so far removed from the contemporary social life that it has but little influence in the world of ordinary men. Consequently the path of educational history from the days of Plato down to the present is literally strewn with theories which have left practice almost unchanged.

The second approach to the study of educational theory, though lacking in precedent, will be followed here. Rather than examine the writings of American educators we shall study the educational institutions which have been evolved in the United

States and shall endeavor to abstract from the actual practice of education the principles to which it gives expression. Through its concrete program of education a nation must give conscious or unconscious answer to every important question of theory, and these practical responses of society, rooted in the folkways and mores of the population, possess a validity and a vitality which no purely theoretic pronouncements, however authoritative, can hope to attain. With some measure of fidelity they must reflect the genius of a given people, the history of a particular civilization, and the conditions of life in a certain natural setting. In a word, they constitute the living theory of education of a country, the theory which has been made flesh and endowed with the breath of life.

Such an exposition of educational theory, however, is beset with difficulties. It will carry the inquiry not only beyond the writings of educators to the institutions of education, but also beyond these institutions to the interplay of social and geographic forces. We shall find that a particular educational form gives expression to a particular theory of life which in turn is the resultant of the operation of numerous natural and human factors. This is peculiarly true in the United States where from the earliest times the conduct and control of education has been in the hands of the people, where, since the settling of the first colonists along the Atlantic seaboard, responsibility for the establishment and maintenance of schools has been for the most part a charge upon the small community. To an unusual degree the development of education in America has been shaped by the desires and aspirations of ordinary men and women. The republic, to be sure, has had its educational leaders who have left their mark upon the system of schools; but these leaders have been effective only as they have organized and given expression to the articulate will of the populace. And they have been political leaders as often as they have been educators in the narrower sense of the term. Indeed the man who above all others is credited by Americans with the founding of their system of public schools, Horace Mann of Massachusetts, was first of all a statesman and a tribune of the people. Thus, while in countries where the administration of schools is highly centralized, the theory of education might perhaps be studied by referring to a few great names or a small number of official documents, in the United States attention must be centered primarily on the changing circumstances and ideals of the American people.

The present approach to educational theory will

not, of course, reveal that logical consistency which is characteristic of a rounded system of thought. Theory which is abstracted from practice is certain to contain numerous contradictions and to lack completeness. It will exhibit all of the characteristics of a living organism: it will possess the vestiges of adaptations to conditions which have passed away, as well as imperfect and partial adjustments to the contemporary situation. Also in response to varying surroundings it will show some differences from community to community. In a country like the United States, with its highly dynamic civilization and its vast areas, these two factors of time and place are peculiarly potent.

The American educational system, as it took form during the first three-quarters of the nineteenth century, reflected the conditions, the ideals, and the aspirations of a pioneering and agrarian society. In this society life was simple, community was isolated from community, human wants were few, the cultural level was low, and a general condition of economic equality and security prevailed. But during the past generation and a half social changes of the most profound character have shattered the old order, and on its ruins there is arising a highly integrated and mechanical civilization which is marked by vast industrial combinations,

minute division of labor, complicated monetary
arrangements, intricate systems of transportation
and communication, concentration of population in
urban centers, wide differences in wealth and income, commercialized amusement and recreation,
the relaxation of moral standards and sanctions, the
disintegration of time-honored institutions, the repudiation of ancient philosophies and theories of
the universe, and the general heightening of the
tension of life. To this new order educational policies and programs have but partially adapted
themselves. They still contain numerous elements
which can be explained only in terms of a civilization which to-day is only a memory.

The United States embraces a territory almost
as great as the whole of Europe west of the Urals,
a territory of widely varying climate and natural
resources. It has its sea coasts, its great mountain
ranges, its fertile river valleys, its broad plains,
and its featureless deserts; it has its forests, its
fisheries, its mineral deposits, its water-falls, its
farm lands, and its pastures. In response to these
differing geographic conditions and the slightly
diverse original cultural impulses, civilization has
assumed somewhat distinctive forms in the several
parts of the country. No one would confuse Puritan New England, even with its industries and its

growing Catholic immigrant population, with any other division of the Union. Likewise on the far Pacific coast in California, in the Rocky Mountain territory, in the farming states of the Middle West, in the expanding industrial area about the Great Lakes, in the mining zones of the Appalachians, in the Southern states of slave-holding tradition, and in the great metropolitan, commercial, and cosmopolitan region centering in New York City indigenous cultures are appearing. To be sure, the processes and instruments of social differentiation and integration—the locomotive, the automobile, and the airplane; the telephone, the telegraph, and the radio; the book press, the daily newspaper, and the periodical journals; the common language, the absence of customs' barriers, and the unity of cultural tradition—all combine to remove differences and to produce a single civilization from the Atlantic to the Pacific and from the Dominion of Canada to the Gulf of Mexico. But diversity of occupation and climate may be expected to bear a cultural fruit. And to-day wide variation in educational practice from area to area in the United States is but one expression of the operation of these different forces.

In spite of these divergences, however, certain broad generalizations regarding the theory underlying the American system of education may be drawn. While perhaps no two minds would agree at all points on the elements composing this theory, there are ten principles which may be singled out for emphasis and which should arouse but little dispute among informed persons. They may be styled the principle of faith in education, the principle of governmental responsibility, the principle of local initiative, the principle of individual success, the principle of democracy, the principle of national solidarity, the principle of social conformity, the principle of mechanical efficiency, the principle of practical utility, and the principle of philosophic uncertainty. Perhaps all of these principles might be stated differently and perhaps others might be added; but a clear grasp of each of these ten generalizations in its applications and in its relations to American life, will open the way to an understanding of the actual theory that motivates education in the United States. The exposition in the present volume will be organized about these ten principles.

CHAPTER II

FAITH IN EDUCATION

PERHAPS the most fundamental of all questions of
educational theory is the question of the power of
the environment over the individual. It has of
course long been a truism among sociologists that
the growth of human culture rests upon the successful transmission of the social heritage from
generation to generation by the two-fold process
of teaching and learning. That in large areas of social life both the teaching and the learning may be
entirely unplanned and incidental to other activities is a matter of no great consequence. The point
of interest here is merely that in the absence of
such a process the accumulation of knowledge, the
building of invention upon invention, the creation
of art, science, and philosophy, and even the development of language itself would be confined
within the narrow limits of individual experience.
Consequently, so long as generations come and go,
so long as birth and death set bounds to the cycle
of life, the mere perpetuation of society and the
survival of man as he is known to history must

depend upon a broad process of education which
reaches into the most remote and intimate corners
of the social order. Such theses regarding the de-
pendence of society as a whole on education require
no defense: they are self-evident. But concerning
the rôle played by the environment in the development of the abilities and the personal traits of the
individual there have been violent disagreements
for centuries. In this controversy the American
people throughout the larger part of their history
as a nation have taken a decided stand.

Popular Faith in the Individual

At the base of the theory of education in the
United States is a profound faith in the potentialities of the individual man. Although this faith
has been severely shaken in recent years by the
advance of industrialism, the appearance of a more
complex social order, the tendencies towards social
stratification, the results of biological and psychological investigation, and the general disenchant-
ment regarding democratic institutions, the Americans continue to believe in the essential equality
of men. They still stoutly affirm in the language
of their radical forefathers that the individual is
a product of the sum total of influences which play

upon him from birth to maturity and that inequalities are to be explained chiefly in terms of differences in opportunity and of injustices perpetuated by social institutions and conventions. This doctrine, which may be traced to the writings of the French philosophers of the period of the Enlightenment, found extreme expression in the American Declaration of Independence in 1776. Moreover, the citizens of the young republic were revolutionists and, like all revolutionists, had unlimited faith in the power of the environment to transform the individual; and, while the inhabitants of contemporary America could scarcely be regarded as revolutionary in either temper or aspiration, they still love to repeat the slogans of their heroic age.

The influence of the Revolution itself, however, would probably have been rapidly dissipated, if it had not been powerfully reënforced by the circumstances of history. The decades immediately following the separation from England witnessed the crossing of the Allegheny Mountains and the swift conquest of the Ohio and Mississippi valleys. Into this virgin and fertile region, uniquely blessed by nature, flowed a never-ending stream of immigrants from the Atlantic states and the countries of Western Europe; and here in an untamed land devoid of historical tradition, where men faced nature with the simplest of tools, whatever artificial social distinctions may have survived the leveling processes of migration rapidly melted away. When a man entered this strange new land he was forced to leave his ancestry and his family connections behind him. His neighbors judged him according to standards set by the needs and conditions of life: they merely wanted to know whether he could hunt and fight and work and endure hardship, whether he was courageous and resourceful and dependable. This was the period of the rifle and the log cabin, of privation and opportunity, of struggle and hope. Representatives from the favored and the exploited classes of the world met on terms of equality, and in some cases the palm of victory went to the one and in some cases to the other. But the broad observation which the Americans themselves have made and which they are fond of dwelling upon is that their history from the days of the first pioneers down to the present is literally crowded with instances of persons of humble origins rising to positions of responsibility and leadership in the affairs of the community, the state, and the nation. Little wonder therefore that the notions regarding the nature of the individual which they had inherited from beyond the Atlantic underwent radical revision. Moreover, it was not mere chance that this revision took place during the first half of the nineteenth century when the common man was coming into his own and beginning to play an active part in the political life of the country. This period also witnessed the laying of the foundations of the American system of public education.

Another powerful argument supporting the Americans in their widespread belief in the importance of environmental influences is found in their history taken as a whole. Indeed the development of the United States in the last century, a development which on the material side is without parallel in the experience of the race, is a tribute to the energy, the capacity, and the character of the common man. From the beginning America has been settled by the poor and oppressed peoples of the world. While the immigrants to the new land have no doubt included many adventurers, gamblers, idealists, non-conformists, and religious dissenters from the favored classes, for the most part they have come from the underprivileged, and even the severely underprivileged, elements in the older societies. What America has achieved therefore stands as a monument to the abilities which were latent in the ignorant and impoverished masses of Europe. Consequently, although in certain circles to-day there may be observed a disposition to emphasize the factor of heredity and to identify innate excellence with those classes which have succeeded according to the accepted American standards, the tradition developed in the days when the republic was young still dominates the educational philosophy of the country.

Popular Faith in the School

This faith in the potentialities of the individual has gradually taken the form of a faith in education. The Americans regard education as the means by which the inequalities among individuals are to be erased and by which every desirable end is to be achieved. Confront practically any group of citizens with a difficult problem in the sphere of human relations and they will suggest education as the solution. Indeed this belief in the general beneficence of education is one of the fetishes of American society. Although the processes of tuition may be but obscurely understood by the popular mind, they are thought to possess something akin to magical power. Perhaps the most striking aspect of this phenomenon, however, lies in the fact that education is identified with the work of the school. As a consequence the faith in education becomes a faith in the school, and the school is looked upon as a worker of miracles. *In fact, the school is the American road to culture.*

The unbounded faith in the school is shown in manifold ways, but there are three lines of evidence which are peculiarly significant. In the first place, the American people display a genuine willingness to provide the material basis of education. While the tax-paying elements in the population have attempted from time to time to halt the growth of school expenditures, their efforts have met with little success. To-day the annual budget for the entire program of education in the United States exceeds two billions of dollars. In the second place, the growth in attendance at the secondary schools, colleges, and universities during the past generation bears eloquent testimony to the popular faith in the school. The expansion of secondary education in particular, to which detailed reference will be made later, reveals the strength of this faith. In the third place, and perhaps most significant of all, the processes of the school are being studied in America to-day on an enormous scale. Since the opening of the present century university departments of education and independent teachers colleges have appeared throughout the country. While perhaps the major function of these institutions is that of professional training, a second function of growing importance is concerned with study, research, and publication.

This exclusive emphasis on the school, however, constitutes a fundamental weakness in the American theory of education. Obviously the school is but one among many educational institutions, and its power can easily be exaggerated. Certainly the American people place too much confidence in what it can do. One need only recall the family, the church, the press, the theater, the cinema, the library, and the museum to realize that the school, if it works alone, can accomplish but little beyond the performance of certain rather definite tasks with which other institutions and the ordinary processes of living are not concerned. And a theory of education which is devoted altogether to what goes on in the school is sure to be lacking in reality and vitality. Particularly in a country like America, where life itself is so complex and where educational agencies of a non-scholastic character are so active, any attempt to erect an educational theory upon such a narrow foundation must of necessity prove timid, unimaginative, and inadequate.

A very genuine evil which flows from this narrow conception of education is a false notion with regard to equality of opportunity. If such equal-

ity is defined in terms of education, and if education is identified with schooling, then the slogan
itself becomes an instrument of deception. Many
Americans seem to believe that the wide extension
of education to the masses—and their achievements in this direction are truly magnificent—
means the general equalization of opportunity.
Clearly to the extent that education is not the
whole of opportunity, and schooling not the whole
of education, such a belief is dangerous and calculated to blind the eyes to social injustice.

In America, therefore, social as well as educational considerations make imperative the revision
and the enlargement of the conception of education. However, in the present work the American
theory of education will be examined as it is and
not as it might or should be. But in order to examine this theory it will first be necessary to present
in brief outline the salient features of the system
of schools as it has developed in the United States.

The American System of Schools

If a generous allowance be made for wide departures from the mode and for certain important
exceptions which will be taken into account later,
the American system of schools may be said to

consist of a single series of institutions maintained at public expense and open to all classes whose members have the disposition and the necessary leisure to attend them. While controlled by the political power, this system is practically independent of the federal authority, and even in the separate states is very largely under the direction of the local communities. In its sequential organization it consists of three levels or divisions: an eight-year elementary school ordinarily enrolling children from six to fourteen years of age, a four-year secondary school, and a four-year college of arts and sciences. Crowning the system are numerous graduate and professional schools with courses of widely varying duration and commonly united with the undergraduate colleges into a more or less loose federation under the name of university. At various points above the elementary school a variety of institutions for vocational training branch off from this main stem. Also in that period which in the past has been known as the pre-school age nursery schools and kindergartens play a minor but increasing rôle; and at the upper age levels numerous agencies for the education of adults are appearing. For the most part, passage from a lower to a higher school, even where the college or university is involved, is not barred by special examination. Probably in part as a consequence of this freedom of movement within the system the enrollment above the elementary school is extraordinarily large. Coeducation of the sexes, which merely means the admission of both boys and girls, men and women, to the same institutions, is the common, though not the universal, practice at all levels of the system and throughout the country. In both the elementary and the secondary schools the great majority of teachers are women and, in comparison with the leading countries of Western Europe, both youthful and poorly trained. Particularly in the great cities and the institutions of higher learning the position of the educational administrator is greatly exalted and the mechanics of educational organization are generally emphasized. The program of instruction is intensely practical, the school is very sensitive to the social demands of influential groups, and education is everywhere regarded in instrumental and utilitarian terms. For the purpose of insuring national solidarity and the perpetuation of the existing social order large emphasis is placed on civic and social education. On the whole the relations in the school among pupils and teachers are free, informal, and democratic. The actual control of education, however, in spite of the democratic political forms which almost universally prevail, rests in the hands of the "educated" and favored social classes.

This highly condensed descriptive statement must of course be regarded at best as only a very rough approximation to the truth. The actual situation, because of the part played by local initiative in the development of schools in America, exhibits little of the simplicity of such a pronouncement. It has been truly said that there is no system of education in the United States. Moreover, under the dynamic conditions of American life, nothing is stable, nothing is permanent: all is change. Thus the so-called traditional system of schools here described, which could scarcely be said to have taken form before the close of the nineteenth century, is cracking at a hundred points under the strain placed upon it by industrial society. To-day it has entered well into a period of radical reorganization which is profoundly modifying its structure. The foregoing account, however, though it may falsify the situation to a degree, will serve to introduce the reader to the study of theory which is to follow.

CHAPTER III

GOVERNMENTAL RESPONSIBILITY

IF the efficacy of educational influences be taken for granted, the most crucial of all educational questions is the question of control. The teacher no doubt is important, and so is the curriculum, as well as many other elements in the program; but there must be some power to select the teacher and to approve the curriculum. In a word both teacher and curriculum must be acceptable to the forces in control. In the last analysis and in all critical matters the school must adopt the philosophy and serve the purposes of the groups or factions in society which hold the reins of actual power. At any rate the school can never for any appreciable period of time oppose with success the insistent demands of such interests. Always, and in the long run, it must conform to their expressed will. Consequently the most significant and profound changes in educational practice and responsible educational theory normally accompany or follow changes in the forces in control.

In America a certain theory of control which

was developed during the period of the agrarian culture and which ignores to a certain extent a number of fundamental questions raised by industrialism, has persisted for so many decades that its validity is accepted as axiomatic. This is the principle that education, conceived as schooling, is a governmental responsibility. Although the forces in control of the government have changed radically during recent generations, the American people as a whole, certain religious denominations excepted, never question this basic principle.

Control by the Political Power

During the seventeenth and eighteenth centuries the control of education in the American colonies was very largely in the hands of the church. To this general rule there were of course many exceptions, but the exceptions were often more apparent than real. In the Massachusetts colony, for example, laws were passed by the general assembly in 1642 and 1647 which recognized the supremacy of the state in educational matters. An examination of the social structure of the colony, however, as well as the dominating preoccupations of the people, reveals a theocracy in which no clear line between church and state is drawn. Therefore, since the religious authority was dominant and since theological interests were the major concern of the time, these early statutes which have ordinarily been interpreted as presaging the development of the great state educational systems of a later age were in reality expressions of the will of the Puritan church. In all of this the American colonies were of course merely following the tradition established on the other side of the Atlantic where the ecclesiastical had long been regarded as superior to the secular power.

In the course of time, partly because of forces operating generally in the western world and partly because of circumstances peculiar to the American situation, the influence of the church in temporal affairs declined. The development of science gradually undermined the dogmas on which the church had rested for ages; the growth of commerce and industry turned the attention of the people to the good things of this world; the development of new means of communication and transportation enriched the experiences and greatly broadened the intellectual horizon of the masses; the popular conquest of the alphabet and the accompanying expansion of the press reduced the range of strictly esoteric knowledge; the increase in the authority of the state occasioned by warfare with Indian tribes and foreign countries correspondingly weakened the prestige of the church; and the breaking of the tie with England and the founding of an independent nation caused politics to displace theology as a center of intellectual interest. All of these forces, as well as many others of less importance, combined to cause the political state to assume responsibility for the organization and conduct of education. This movement towards secular control reached its initial fruition in the first half of the nineteenth century when in the more progressive states of the Union great systems of public education were founded. And the principle having been once established, its universal adoption throughout the nation was merely a question of time.

Although the motives which led the American people to make education a state function were diverse and even conflicting, the theory underlying the practice to-day is fairly clear. In the first place, as the state superseded the church as the dominant force in society it became interested in the making of good citizens, just as the church in its time had been interested in the saving of souls and the making of good communicants. Regarding the nature of the good citizen, however, the Americans have never been in full agreement. At one time they emphasize the element of loyalty, and at another the element of intelligence; at one time the passive, and at another the active virtues. Moreover, since the founding of the republic, and particularly since the adoption of universal manhood suffrage, men have quite logically contended that the safety of the state requires an educated citizenry.

From the standpoint of the commonweal education is therefore so important that it cannot be left to the uncertainties of private enterprise. But here again as to whether the safety of the state is best guarded by instilling into the citizens a more or less blind worship of the forms of government created by the fathers or by preparing them to criticize intelligently all existing institutions, to regard all elements of the social structure as more or less provisional, and to work constantly for the reconstruction and improvement of society is a question to which diverse answers are given. On the whole, at least in the sphere of the relation of education to politics, the more conservative view seems to have prevailed. Although certain of America's leading educational thinkers to-day take the position that the school should serve as a leavening and creative force in the social order, the people as a whole lack the revolutionary spirit of their ancestors. They believe firmly that the state should control the schools for the purpose of making good citizens; but they regard the good citizen as the man or woman who reveres the names of the founding fathers, accepts the American form of government as almost divinely ordered, and performs honestly and efficiently, but unimaginatively, the routine tasks of civic life.

A second motive for making education a function of the state which historically has made a powerful appeal to the American people is that of equalizing opportunity among the classes. Viewing education in the form of schooling as an opportunity of almost transcendent worth, they feel that the state alone is sufficiently powerful to organize and maintain a system of schools which will reach the entire population. A single reference to the history of education in the United States will be sufficient to support this thesis. The fight for the great state systems of education, though often led by intellectuals and the more enlightened members of favored classes, was carried to a successful conclusion by the votes of the underprivileged masses. And to-day these masses regard the public school with a strong and sustained affection and look upon it as a charter of their liberties.

A Secularized Program of Instruction

The Americans believe not only that the control of education should rest with the political power but also that the program of instruction in the public schools should be secularized. In taking this position they have likewise departed radically from the doctrines of their more distant ancestors. The schools of the colonial period were almost everywhere strongly sectarian in bias. In fact practically everything taught in the curriculum, even spelling and arithmetic and science, was made to serve some religious purpose. To-day, at least in the opinion of the ordinary citizen, religion plays, and should play, no part in the instruction in the public school. This institution, like its parent the state, is supposed to be neutral in religious matters and to leave all forms of religious tuition to the family and the church.

The reason for this separation of school and church was less a product of political theorizing than a response to a practical situation. Although traditionally America has been Christian, and preponderantly Protestant Christian, since colonial times she has also been a land of the greatest sectarian diversity. In the United States to-day there are seven different denominations with more than one million adherents each. Moreover, no one denomination is sufficiently powerful, by reason of either historical tradition or present numerical strength, to shape the situation in its own interests. Consequently, since no single church is able to get its own program accepted in the schools, and since every church tends to regard the teachings of its rivals as more dangerous than no religious instruction whatsoever, the inevitable result has been a compromise: the public school has been forced to follow a policy of neutrality among the warring religious sects.

The secularization of the school program, however, has not met with universal support. The Catholic Church, for example, whose strength has grown with the coming of immigrants from the Catholic countries of Europe, has never conceded to the state the right to educate and has consequently sought to organize and maintain schools of its own. And various of the Protestant sects, as they have witnessed the decay of religious belief and the decline of the church as an educational force in community life, have advanced numerous proposals for bringing about some articulation between church and public school. Moreover, certain radical elements in society have contended that the refusal on the part of the school to deal with problems which are styled religious represents a cowardly evasion of responsibility. They argue that the school should face these problems squarely and honestly and should help the coming generation to reconstruct its outlook on life in the light of the findings of science and the whole range of human experience. Under existing conditions they contend that the school inadvertently lends its support to the perpetuation of superstition and obscurantism.

In these various criticisms the American people as a whole show little interest. On the one hand, they have a deep-seated fear of permitting the church to establish any organic connection with the institutions of public education. They recall the bitter sectarian disputes of an earlier age and are inclined to regard religion as a divisive force in the school. On the other hand, they feel that the religious influence in education is likely to be narrow in scope and conservative in spirit. They point to the impoverished curriculum of the school in the days of church control and to the primitive methods of instruction that still prevail so largely in educational agencies under ecclesiastical management. They also argue that the church, because of the irrational quality in its foundations, is by nature a most conservative institution and slow to respond to the demands of society. Being essentially a practical people they desire a school that is progressive and sensitive to the facts of social change. All of these considerations tend to confirm the American people in their present practice.

The observation should be made, however, that this neutrality with respect to the religious question is only partial and superficial. In spite of the theoretical separation of church and school there are many public schools in the United States to-day in which religious rites, such as prayer, psalm-singing, and the reading of sacred scripture, are conducted as part of the daily or weekly program. This is due to the fact that the American people are after all steeped in an intensely religious tradition. Consequently, where conditions permit, the religious influence tends to find its way into the school. And such conditions are fulfilled wherever the community supporting the school is overwhelmingly of one denomination or creed. In a community of this type instruction with a religious bias, and with the particular bias of the denomination in power, will be introduced into the school as a matter of course and without organized opposition. In the more simple, rural, and industrially retarded areas in America such homogeneity is a common condition.

In a yet more profound and important sense the program of the American public school everywhere is religious. Although the system of beliefs evolved through the centuries by the Christian Church is apparently passing into dissolution, the American people still very generally believe in the existence of a supernatural order which underlies the order of nature and which possesses greater reality than the world of sense. This Christian ethic, though modified at many points, tends to permeate the program of instruction of the entire system of public education. In the readers used in the elementary school, in the literature and history at the secondary level, and to some extent even in the philosophy and ethics of the college and university there is a general tendency to accept and to lend support to the view of the universe which has been identified with historical Christianity. Moreover, the Americans very commonly employ the term Christian as a term of approbation. They speak approvingly of a good Christian girl, a sound Christian character, a Christian community, a Christian nation, or a Christian civilization. And among them the highest of compliments is to say that an individual possesses the Christian virtues.

In the influence of all of this on the program of
the school, there is of course no conscious planning. The American people are merely reflecting
the history through which they have passed.

Toleration of Private Enterprise

One of the most interesting and significant features of the American theory of education is the
place which it gives to private initiative. As we
have already observed, education in the United
States was originally in the hands of the church
and non-public agencies. Although the relative importance of private enterprise has steadily declined
since the state assumed responsibility for education, to-day private enterprise in the field of education is tolerated and even encouraged throughout
practically the entire nation.

The rôle, however, which private enterprise
plays varies greatly from region to region in the
country and from level to level in the educational
system. In the East and in the more long-settled
areas generally the tradition of the private school
naturally exhibits greatest strength. This tradition
is also strong wherever the Roman Catholics, as
well as the adherents of certain minor religious
denominations, have congregated in large numbers.

In the nation as a whole both the elementary and the secondary schools are predominantly under public direction, while in the realm of higher education private institutions still carry the larger burden. Thus, less than ten per cent. of the elementary and secondary school pupils are attending private schools, whereas the corresponding percentage in the institutions of higher education, excluding normal schools and teachers colleges, is well above sixty. If the influence of the religious factor be disregarded, private enterprise remains strongest in those portions of the United States and at those levels of the educational system where the more favored social classes have sent down their deepest roots.

In support of their policy of tolerating and encouraging private enterprise in the field of education the Americans advance two major arguments. In the first place, they say that there are limits to which the state should go in determining the content of education. They seem to feel that parents have certain rights over the education of the child which the state must respect. While granting that the state may be justified in preventing private schools from teaching doctrines which are inimical to its own welfare and in setting up minimum standards of achievement which all schools must enforce, they maintain that there are certain matters of conscience in which the state must not interfere. In other words, the fear and mistrust of governments which played such an important part in their own revolution survive to this day. It is interesting to observe, however, that during periods of great national crisis the instrumentalities of government which were designed to safeguard the rights of the individual are generally violated.

In the second place, the Americans contend that the toleration of private enterprise tends to encourage experimentation and the discovery of new methods. Undoubtedly, where the entire educational program is obedient to one authority, there is grave danger that a single point of view will be supported everywhere, that this point of view will be in essential harmony with the routine of tradition, and that new ideas will be dismissed without a hearing. The history of education in America, moreover, does record innumerable instances of experiments conducted and tested by private enterprise. Where these experiments have proved fruitful and in accord with the prevailing social philosophy, they have often been incorporated into the system of public education. This of course does not prove conclusively that there is no other method of securing experimentation. It merely proves that in America, with the particular set of social institutions found there, this method has been found effective.

Another argument in favor of private enterprise which plays some part in the American theory is the contention that it provides an excellent opportunity for men of great wealth to devote a portion of their substance to the service of the public. Sometimes the argument takes the other form that a society should have rich men in order that it may secure patrons of great universities, art galleries, and other cultural undertakings which the people themselves would be unwilling to support. According to the assumption underlying this theory, in the absence of millionaires the arts and the sciences would languish. Certainly in America the tradition of turning private funds to such uses has developed great strength, and huge fortunes are given to educational enterprises every year. The extent, however, to which this tradition affects the policies of the universities receives but little attention at the hands of the American people. Occasionally the board of trustees of some institution refuses a donation on high moral grounds, but as a rule the gift is gladly received and devoted to the purposes determined upon by the donor. In view of the fact that the great body of citizens regard

the pursuit of wealth as a perfectly normal and
legitimate occupation of man, to expect a more
critical attitude towards this practice would be irrational and Utopian.

Dominant Forces in American Society

In concluding this discussion of the principle of
governmental responsibility a word should be said
regarding the dominant forces in American society.
It is not sufficient to say that education is a function
of the state, or even that the state rests upon a
wide popular franchise. In societies with democratic
political forms, as well as in others, effective power
may be highly concentrated in certain favored
groups. In the control of education in the United
States this would seem clearly to be the case.

During the colonial period of American history
education was to a very large degree in the hands
of the clergy. Following this early phase and before the rise of the new industrial civilization, at
least at the lower levels of the system, the masses
of the people, represented chiefly by farmers, seem
to have been in control. To-day, both the clergy
and the farmers are out of the picture, and educational policy is determined for the most part by
members of the favored urban classes—leaders in

the industrial, mercantile, and intellectual life of the nation. Thus the ordinary board of education in the United States is very commonly composed of manufacturers, merchants, managers, lawyers, physicians, and occasional representatives from other occupational groups. Very rarely, except in the small rural communities, is a manual laborer or a direct representative of the masses elected to membership on the board.

While this situation has called forth some criticism from labor and radical sources, it is quite generally accepted as desirable by students of school administration and by the American people generally. They contend that in many of its aspects the conduct of education is a form of business enterprise; that this enterprise is conducted most efficiently by persons accustomed to the handling of large affairs; and that the desired qualities are likely to be possessed in most abundant measure by the types of men and women who to-day dominate the board of education. For a carpenter or a mechanic to participate in the deliberations of a body concerned with the administration of an institution of higher learning would seem to them peculiarly incongruous. They naturally feel that the control of education should be delegated to those who have had the fullest possible cultural advantages and who have been most successful according to the standards set by American society. That these persons in their deliberations will place the common good above the interests of their own class is confidently assumed.

CHAPTER IV

LOCAL INITIATIVE

CLOSELY related to the question of governmental responsibility is that of the size of the political division which should exercise control over education. In facing this issue different peoples have given the most diverse answers. Some have centralized power in the national capital; others have invested the local community with very large authority; and yet others have pursued various courses of intermediate character. Just what policy should be followed here is a question of paramount importance, because the relation of education to politics is involved in the answer.

The American people, at least in the past, have placed their faith in an extreme form of local initiative. No one therefore can understand their system of education without first understanding the very fundamental rôle which the small community plays in the support and control of the schools. The first impression which the student of education, who knows only the highly centralized systems of continental Europe, gathers from an examination of the American program is one of extreme bewilderment. Even persons who have devoted years to the study of education in the United States hesitate to speak with assurance concerning practice in the nation as a whole.

The Weakness of the Federal Government

When the American Union was formed in the latter part of the eighteenth century the thirteen colonies which entered into the federation regarded themselves as independent states and were exceedingly jealous of their sovereignty. It was in fact only with the greatest difficulty and by means of shrewd political manipulation that they were persuaded to relinquish a portion of this sovereignty and accept membership in the union. In those days there was a general mistrust of any government far removed from the communities governed; moreover, whether that government was located in London or in some American city seemed to many a sturdy champion of local rights a matter of little importance. As a consequence the powers of the federal government were carefully listed in the written constitution, which formed the basis of the union, and, according to the provisions of the tenth amendment to this document, all other powers were reserved to the individual states. Since education was not mentioned in the constitution, it thus came to be regarded as an exclusive interest of the separate commonwealths.

The federal government, to be sure, has not altogether ignored the problem of education. As early as 1787 it provided for the setting aside of public lands in the West for the support of schools; in 1862 it passed the famous Morrill Act which founded the colleges of agriculture and mechanic arts in the different states; in 1867 it created a Department of Education at Washington which in 1869 was reduced to a bureau and in 1929 to an office in the Department of the Interior; and through various other measures it has manifested an interest in public education and even a desire to exercise some measure of administrative control. In recent years numerous campaigns with powerful support have been launched to found a federal department of education with large functions, but thus far these efforts have not met with success. Consequently, education in the United States remains to-day essentially a function of the forty-eight separate commonwealths. With this general principle the American people are in relatively complete agreement. Even those who advocate the establishment of a department of education at

Washington are careful to insist that the particular proposals which they advance will not infringe upon the rights of the states.

This opposition to federal control no doubt rests in part on a traditional and irrational mistrust of government, but it also has the support of solid argument. According to the American point of view, education is too powerful an instrument to place in the hands of any single authority. They fear that the central government, if it had administrative control over the schools, might fall under the influence of some unscrupulous minority and that the entire educational system from one end of the country to the other might be employed to keep this minority in power and to indoctrinate the coming generation with a social philosophy inimical to the common good. Moreover, they contend that the present condition of state autonomy, because of its stimulation of experimentation and variety of effort, is the best possible guarantee of a steady advance in the theory and practice of education. In the forty-eight states there are forty-eight systems of education; and the absence of customs' barriers, the presence of a common language, the ease of communication, and the mobility of the population all combine to facilitate the rapid circulation of ideas. The lines which divide one political division from another thus have no parallel in the cultural realm. The launching of a new educational experiment in one state will therefore become quickly known and observed in others. As a consequence, under their system, so the Americans argue, nowhere can either practice or theory crystallize into rigid and unchanging forms.

The situation has its unpleasant side, however. The contrasts among the states are enormous. In the development of its school system one state may be a generation behind another. The case of secondary education will serve as an illustration. One of the most advanced states, such as California, may have four times as large a proportion of its children in the high school as some state at the other end of the scale, such as Arkansas or Mississippi. Moreover, the ability to support education varies greatly from state to state. Thus, according to a federal report for 1918, the amount of taxable wealth for each pupil in school ranged from slightly more than $2,500 in Mississippi, to almost $40,000 in Nevada. Obviously the children in the very poor areas are victims of the American policy of local autonomy. And since, under the conditions of close economic integration which prevail in the United States, no one can say with precision what part of the wealth resident in one state is the product of local efforts, this practice of making the support of schools follow state lines is highly arbitrary and probably involves great social injustice. Many educators are consequently wondering whether the American people may not be paying too heavy a price for the tradition of complete state autonomy in educational affairs.

The Central Rôle of the Local Community

But when the observation has been made that there are forty-eight different state systems of education in America, only a fraction of the picture has been disclosed. Even within the state the local community rather than the central authority has always played the major rôle in the control, support, and conduct of public education. As late as the middle of the last century public education practically everywhere was a function of the school district; and this district may be defined as the smallest possible unit capable of supporting a one-room school with a single poorly trained teacher and the most modest type of equipment. As the inefficiencies of this system became apparent and as the structure of American society took on a more complicated pattern, a reaction against such a policy of administrative anarchy slowly got under way. State departments of education were created and larger units for the conduct of schools were established. To-day, however, in spite of almost a century of growth these central departments commonly exercise but little authority, and even the district system still persists in wide rural areas. Here and there, to be sure, the authority of the state has become a real factor in administration; but as a general rule, within the limits of certain broad provisions requiring the establishment and maintenance of a system of public schools, the local community, and quite frequently a very small local community, is responsible for the support and control of public education.

Although the district system in its extreme form has few defenders among educational leaders in America to-day, the general principle of decentralization receives wide support. The arguments are much the same as those advanced in favor of limiting the power of the federal government in educational affairs. It insures variety in practice, elasticity in organization, and freedom for experimentation. It also brings the school into intimate contact with the people and develops in them a genuine interest in education. This particular feature of the American system will be examined in more detail in a subsequent paragraph.

The placing of such heavy responsibilities upon the local community, however, has its grave disadvantages. Among the various communities within a particular state the inequalities in wealth are even greater than among the states. The inevitable consequence is the extraordinary inequality of educational opportunity and the striking contrasts between schools which every foreign observer is quick to note. The various communities compete with each other on very uneven terms for educational leadership. In this competition the larger and more wealthy communities naturally have an advantage and are thus able to secure the more gifted, the better trained, and the more experienced teachers and administrators. Moreover, under this system promotion usually means passing from a poorer to a richer, from a smaller to a larger community. The rural schools are therefore poorly equipped, poorly taught, and poorly led. The American method of supporting and controlling education, like so many other features of American civilizations, seems to be admirably designed to enable the city to profit at the expense of the country.

Control of Education by the People

The fact has already been observed that under the extreme decentralization of authority which prevails in America the actual control of education rests with the people. It has always been so. Education in the United States has never come down from above. First as colonists along the Atlantic coast and later as pioneers in the wilderness of the interior, the people carried their institutions with them. It was in this way that they established their schools, each community or settlement doing as it saw fit. No great statesman or committee of wise men designed the American system of education. With whatever merits or defects it may possess, it is the genuine handiwork of the people. Almost universally the conduct of elementary and secondary schools is in the hands of local boards of education composed of members chosen in some fashion by the citizens of the community. The boards which control the higher schools and universities are ordinarily somewhat further removed from the citizens, but even here, at least in the case of institutions of public education, the contact is fairly close.

On the whole the Americans favor this practice.

They say that, on the one side, it arouses popular interest in the schools, and, on the other, makes the schools sensitive to social demand. Certainly public education in the United States is firmly rooted in the affections of the masses and has been unusually quick to respond to the needs of society as those needs have been conceived by the chosen representatives of the people. The school is thus given a degree of vitality which it has so commonly lacked during its long and varied history. Moreover, the democratic quality, as well as other genuine merits in the American system of education, may be traced directly to the influence of the people.

The theory of popular control, however, as tested by experience, is not without its shortcomings. The American school reflects the vices as well as the virtues of the American people. The low standards of scholarship, for example, which have commonly characterized educational practice in the United States, may be traced to the fact that ordinary men and women have controlled the school. And the American tradition of putting trust in the untrained teacher is to be understood in the same way. The relatively uncultured pioneers and farmers who have shaped the policies of the public school in the past have been quite content to identify learning with literacy and to rate a teacher as well-trained if he could read, write, and manipulate numbers with some degree of facility. To them an elaborate form of professional training has seemed entirely unnecessary and superfluous. To-day, because the people themselves have reached a higher level of educational attainments and because new social classes are coming into power, they are beginning to demand teachers of higher qualification. But the point to be observed is that the school must inevitably exhibit the cultural limitations as well as the ideals and purposes of the forces in control.

Another consequence of the popular control of the school is that education will be affected by those gusts of passion which from time to time sweep through the masses. Thus, at the time of the Great War the teaching of German was prohibited in a very large proportion of the secondary schools of the United States. Even in the universities the Germanic department suffered enormous reductions in enrollment and occasional dismissals of faculty members. A little later in the city of Chicago, as a part of the reaction from the Anglophile tendencies of the war period, history textbooks were ostentatiously thrown out of the schools because of their alleged British sympathies. At about the same time in certain rural areas, as an expression of a wave of theological fundamentalism which was agitating the culturally more retarded regions, the teaching of evolution was barred from the schools by legislative enactment and a number of teachers of science lost their positions.

The foreign observer, witnessing these instances of mob behavior, comes to the conclusion that the level of culture in the United States must be extremely primitive. The fact is that such manifestations are merely the natural fruit of the way in which public education in America is controlled. The intellectual classes, to whose care education is entrusted by tradition in the older countries of Europe, have but little to say about the conduct of the public school in the United States. Probably in no country in the world do the masses of the people believe in the theory of biological evolution, but in America those masses sit in judgment on educational policy. Thus a price must be paid for the democratization of the control of education.

Administrative Decentralization

The weakness of the federal government in education and the absence of strong central departments in the separate states naturally imply a highly decentralized form of administrative organization. But this question is so important that it merits separate treatment. Moreover, it is at this point in particular that two opposing theories of education are coming in conflict in America to-day, the one representing the rural civilization of the past and the other the new industrial civilization which is rapidly transforming the social order. For the most part the older tradition still prevails, but all the forces of the age appear to be pulling in the other direction.

The administration of public education in America has always been local in character. The federal government has practically no machinery for administering education, and most of the states are without such machinery. This means that as a rule education is administered on the spot rather than from some central office. The consequence is a still further stimulation to variety in standards, procedures, and ideals.

The Americans are generally inclined to regard their practice of decentralization as one of the great merits of their system of education. It means an absence of the bureaucracy, the red tape, and the formal rigidity which so often characterize the administration of public education. The visitor to American schools is impressed by the ease with which he can gain access to persons in authority and secure permission to observe classes or examine records. The source of power is always near at hand. Decentralization also gives to the educational program, paradoxical as it may seem, both a highly dynamic and an extremely stable quality. Methods of teaching, materials of instruction, and institutional structures are constantly changing; new devices, procedures, and theories are sure to be given trial somewhere; even teachers who are dismissed from one school may find employment in another. Yet, unless the people as a whole are moved by some powerful passion, there can be no sudden and sweeping change of a radical nature in the educational program of the nation, because there is no one center through which that program in its entirety can be reached. The American school system is a loosely articulated system of diverse institutions scattered over a vast country. Its inertia is consequently tremendous.

Another product of decentralization which the Americans value greatly is the stimulus which it has given to the development of teachers colleges and university departments of education where the nature and the problems of education can be studied. In the absence of all-powerful ministries of education the formulation of policies has gradually passed to these institutions; and it is in them rather than in administrative offices that real leadership in education in the United States resides. The Americans argue, moreover, that under their system theories and programs, being evolved in centers of inquiry which are remote from the play of social forces, must win their way in the practical field on the basis of their merits rather than because of the more or less arbitrary exercise of power by some influential personality or group of politicians. Also, since these theories and programs are the natural fruit of investigation and discussion, they rest upon a much more substantial foundation than the formulations of a department or ministry of education.

The extreme decentralization of educational administration in America, however, leads to much waste and incoördination. It possesses the defects of its merits. Thus, there is no machinery for introducing quickly and effectively into the entire system of education the thoroughly tested results of educational science. Before the battle for progress is completely won it must be fought on a thousand fronts, it must be carried to every center of authority in the country. Then there is the great variety of procedure, a variety without reason or philosophy, which so hampers the coördination of institution with institution. The population in the United States is highly mobile. Families are constantly on the move: they move from community to community, from state to state, and from one end of the nation to the other. The absence of common standards and common practices in the schools results in much hardship to the pupils involved. A similar difficulty arises when students enter college or university from different lower schools. They bring to the higher institution most diverse forms of preparation. The result, so the opponents of decentralization affirm, is educational waste and inefficiency.

The discussion thus far has quite rightly emphasized the feature of administrative decentralization. It should be noted, however, that this feature of the American educational system is the very obvious product of the old agrarian order which was itself highly decentralized in character and which is now rapidly passing away. In that order community was isolated from community, modern methods of transportation and communication were absent, and society lacked the means of integration. To-day a totally new type of society is appearing; and it is altogether possible, if not probable, that the traditional system of decentralized administration will gradually be superseded by a system of an opposite character. In the large cities, as will be pointed out in another section of this volume, the new order has already appeared. Whether it will survive and spread is of course uncertain, but it has its defenders among educational theorists.

Institutional Autonomy

The American policy of decentralization, of encouraging local initiative, and of tolerating private enterprise, has given birth to a condition of institutional autonomy at the upper levels of the educational system that deserves special attention. For the country as a whole there is no provision for the coördination of the work of the universities and professional schools and for the subordination of a particular institution to some unified plan. Even within the boundaries of a single state such a plan, affecting both public and private schools, is universally lacking. Each institution is commonly a law unto itself and engages in a competitive struggle with its neighbors for funds, students, professors, and departments. The consequence is an enormous amount of duplication of effort and failure to articulate with the needs of society. The number of persons being trained for a particular profession, for example, may bear but little relation to the social need, because the Americans have developed no machinery designed to measure this need and no machinery for coördinating the efforts of the various training institutions involved. Moreover, under their policy a particular region may be supporting a half dozen centers for providing a certain type of instruction where one center would be ample. Even the library facilities on some highly erudite subject may be scattered through a number of universities instead of being concentrated at the one point where they would be of maximum usefulness.

The American people, however, are quite prepared to defend this practice, except perhaps in its most extreme form. This defense no doubt rests in part on the somewhat naïve postulate that no society can have too many of any type of educational agency or too much of any kind of education. More fundamental is the firm belief in the general beneficence of the principle of competition in the realm of higher education, as well as in the world of industry. In fact their entire system of education from top to bottom, with its emphasis on decentralization and local initiative, is defended on the grounds that it prevents the universal adoption of any single practice, theory of education, or system of thought, and brings them all into free competition. Moreover, they like to think of their country as a vast testing ground where the most diverse educational ideas meet on equal terms. They consequently argue that, with all of the waste, incoördination, and apparent aimlessness which characterize their educational program, they are building on a more solid foundation than those peoples who endeavor to follow a preconceived plan. The way in which this predisposition affects the fundamental relationships between school and society and the formulation of a general theory of education will be considered in the closing chapter of the present volume.

CHAPTER V

INDIVIDUAL SUCCESS

THERE is no principle that is more characteristic of the American theory and mode of life and that has played a larger rôle in shaping the development of the American educational system than the principle of individual success. Even democracy tends to be identified with a species of individualism and the good society is regarded as one in which the individual is given an opportunity to succeed. Eminent statesmen and university presidents, as well as more humble citizens, vie with each other in praising the social order which permits individuals to rise above the station into which they are born. To the Americans the world is an arena and life is a race. And they are less inclined to inquire after the nature of the stakes than they are to ask whether the conditions are fair and the best man wins. They of course are ready to grant that wide differences in wealth give advantages to certain individuals and handicaps to others, but they are convinced that in America the race is more nearly fair than it has ever been before in human history. Undoubtedly America to-day is a land of great opportunity and the individual of talent, provided his gifts are in harmony with social tradition, is likely to succeed.

The Origin of the Worship of Individual Success

The explanation of this emphasis on individual success is found in the mode of settlement and development of the country. In comparison with the older land areas of the world America was peopled in a very peculiar way. From the earliest times immigrants came to the new continent as individuals, and as individuals they moved westward to the Pacific. Even the socializing influence of the village rarely served to soften the egoistic impulses of the individual: in rural America, and most of America was rural until quite recent times, there are few villages: each family lives on its own farm and looks with a trace of suspicion or distrust at the nearest neighbor half a mile away. Consequently, when these sturdy individualists fashioned their institutions of government, they were greatly concerned about guarding their rights and insuring to themselves and their children the opportunity to succeed.

Competition, however, is certain to go on in any society. The more important question therefore pertains to the prizes which motivate the struggle. Although during the period immediately following the founding of the Union eminence in politics was looked upon with most covetous eyes and every American boy was told that he might become President of the United States, the primary urge which has moved Americans to display that restless energy so characteristic of them has been the desire for economic advancement. Where hundreds or perhaps thousands came to America for religious and political reasons, millions came to improve their economic position. And after their arrival the conditions of life and the very atmosphere of the new world directed their attention increasingly towards the attainment of material success. They found themselves in a country in which the achievement of riches on a fabulous scale was within the realm of possibility. A virgin continent with unlimited natural resources lay before them, an advanced economic technique was in their hands, and because of the rapidity with which the country was being populated mere priority of arrival often insured the automatic acquisition of wealth. As the range and magnitude of the opportunities became apparent in the middle of the nineteenth century, there occurred, at least among the more energetic and ambitious, a mad scramble for lands, forests, mines, and franchises which has continued almost to the present day. Again and again men have seen their friends and relatives acquire huge fortunes in a few years through some lucky chance, bold adventure, unusual prescience, or unscrupulous manipulation. Even the very poor in America therefore cherish the secret hope that either they or their children will sooner or later be ranked among the fortunate. The coming of an elaborate money economy has perhaps accentuated this concentration on the accumulation of wealth. The ideal of individual success has consequently come to be defined in terms of material advancement.

Free Schools

Concern over the equalization of opportunity has been one of the most natural and significant consequences of the emphasis on individual success. While this concern has never influenced the Americans to think seriously of making a direct attack upon the rights of private property, it has caused them to seek in various ways to abate the more deleterious effects of this institution. The founding of a system of free schools represents one such effort. Although many other factors conspired to establish the principle that property should be taxed for the support of education, the general desire to give the individual a chance played a central rôle. Attempts during the colonial period to meet the situation by providing *pauper* schools, that is, schools which children could attend at public expense by proving themselves paupers, violated the American regard for equality of opportunity. Attendance at a *pauper* school obviously tended to place a stamp of inferiority upon the individual.

The founding of free schools, however, obviously does not equalize educational opportunity. Many children, after reaching the age of possible self-support, cannot afford the leisure which the further pursuit of education entails. Thus, in the absence of maintenance grants provided by the state, even in such a rich country as the United States, poverty must continue to restrict the opportunities of schooling. The American people, however, are not prepared to-day to extend such grants to needy children, partly because they think that aid of this type, being selective and not universal, would tend to *pauperize* its recipients, and partly because they feel that the value of opportunity at the upper levels of the system is somewhat reduced if the individual is not required to make some economic sacrifice for it. This conviction, however, has received no practical application in the case of the sons and daughters of the well-to-do classes who receive the most luxurious educational privileges without making the slightest personal sacrifice of any kind.

The Educational Ladder

The pride of the American school system and a major contribution to the advance of civilization is the educational ladder. This ladder, composed of the elementary school, the secondary school, and the state university, constitutes a continuous and unbroken program of instruction from early childhood to maturity and from the first beginnings of school education to the most advanced forms of professional training and graduate study. If the influence of family fortune and tradition be disregarded, the individual in his progress up this ladder encounters no barrier beyond the increasing difficulty of the ascent and the limitations set by his own capacities. The entire range of institutions involved is supported by the state, and any individual able to meet the very modest scholastic requirements enforced is free to attend.

That this arrangement of the institutions of public education represents an almost perfect response to the American interest in opening the way to individual success is suggeste l by the very term by which it has come to be known. When one thinks of a ladder one envisages a movement from lower to higher levels and the conquest of physical obstacles. And the American educational ladder reaches downward to the very lowest strata of society and upward to the most coveted social positions. Although the American people have perhaps overrated the part which the school can play in this elevation and degradation of individuals in the social scale, they regard their system of education as the safest guarantee against that rigid stratification of society which characterizes many of the older civilizations. Times without number, moreover, they have witnessed individuals climbing from one social level to another apparently by means of the educational ladder.

The faith which the American people have in this feature of their educational system has been given vivid expression during the past generation in the expansion of the secondary schools. In 1890 there were probably not more than 300,000 boys and girls in the four-year secondary schools of the nation; to-day the number cannot be far from five millions. For the country as a whole more than one-half, and in many communities practically all, of the children of appropriate age are in high school. Within the last ten years, moreover, the colleges and universities have begun to grow at a correspondingly rapid rate. This upward surge of the masses into the higher levels of the educational structure, which can only be regarded in the nature of a profound social movement, seems to be motivated primarily by a desire for individual success. At great sacrifice parents struggle to "give their children an education" so that they may be freed from the necessity of earning their livelihood by means of physical labor. It is an interesting fact that the people in the United States, while constantly speaking of the dignity of labor and professing to view all forms of labor as equally worthy, seek to escape from its manual varieties as rapidly and completely as possible. And the relative ease with which this escape can be made under the American system, combined with the general condition of material prosperity which prevails, has made practically impossible the development of a revolutionary temper among the masses.

Belief in the Money Value of Schooling

The crowding into the upper divisions of the educational system has no doubt been stimulated by a widespread belief that attendance at school has definite financial value. A few years ago a number of investigations were made which purported to show that every day spent in high school or college increases one's income by so many dollars and cents. These studies were based upon data received from persons who had attended school for varying periods of time. It was found that those who had remained in school longest were receiving the largest incomes and that there is a positive relationship between length of school attendance and earning power. The conclusion drawn was that this relationship is causal in character. The fact that persons attending higher institutions are selected from the standpoint of both native ability and social advantage and the further fact that the training provided by high school and college has in the past possessed the sales advantage of scarcity were both overlooked.

The point of major interest here, however, is not that the American people generally accepted the economics of this analysis, but rather that they accepted its ethics. The assumption that educational opportunities, provided at public expense, should be judged in terms of their money value to the person receiving them reveals the extent to which the new pecuniary order and the ideal of individual success have come to dominate their theory of education. In no earlier generation in America would such a conception of the function of the school have received so uncritical a reception. That public education, even at those levels where attendance is highly restricted, should be regarded essentially as an individual right can perhaps be understood only in terms of that social philosophy which teaches that the general good is best conserved by permitting and even encouraging all men to pursue their own selfish interests.

The Opposition to Specialization in the High School

An observer, unfamiliar with the American system of education, on examining the program of the secondary school would conclude that large provision for intensive specialization is being made in this institution. He would find numerous curricula carrying vocational titles, such as cooking, sewing, animal husbandry, carpentry, journalism, printing, and so on. Superficially this would appear to be an elaborate program of specialized training. On a closer examination of the facts, however, he would find that he was in error. The subjects offered do indeed cover a very wide range, but they are not organized into those extended sequences which are essential to specialization, or at least the sequences, if organized, are not effectively followed. The students tend to experiment with this field and with that, and in the course of the allotted time they collect a sufficient number of *credits* or *points* to graduate. To be sure, this process of dipping here and there is commonly guarded by regulatory measures, but the very frequent result is a scattering of student energies.

The fundamental explanation of this practice is found in the desire of the American people to protect the individual. They have resolutely refused to enforce the pursuit of long sequences below the college and university levels. They have rather supported the theory that their children should be permitted to shift their educational and occupational choices from time to time without loss of academic standing. Every parent nourishes the hope that through some chance turn of the wheel of fortune he will be able to send his boy or girl to college. At the time the child enters the secondary school the possibility of realizing this hope may appear very remote. He consequently may decide in the interests of expediency to encourage the pupil to elect one of the more practical courses. But later, if circumstances should change and he should be able to send the child to college, he would resent bitterly any effort on the part of the educational authorities to require the pupil to begin a new series of sequences in the first year of the high school.

In justification of the parents in this situation American educators have evolved the interesting theory that from the standpoint of preparation for work in the higher schools the important consideration is not the content of the course pursued but rather the method by which the pupil works. A common saying is that the important consideration is not *what* but *how* the individual studies. This doctrine in certain of its interpretations and applications has tended to shatter the psychological foundations on which the older principle of subject-matter sequences had been established. It also represents a triumph of the individual over the demands of society.

The System of Marks, Credits, and Degrees

Motivation in the American public school has rested primarily on an appeal to individual self-interest. In order to stimulate the pupil to achieve, an elaborate system of marks, credits, and degrees which penetrates into practically every level and division of the system of education has been evolved. In order to secure the right to promotion in the elementary school, the points necessary for graduation in the high school, and the academic credits required for the various degrees conferred by the college and the university, the pupil receives marks on his work from week to week, month to month, semester to semester, and year to year throughout his school career. Although various forms of socialized work are gradually appearing, the school relationship continues to be very largely a relationship between the teacher and the pupil.

The major object of various efforts to refine methods of marking seems to be that of meting out to the individual child precisely what he has earned in the form of credits. The Dalton plan, for example, though repudiating certain features of the traditional system, is an admirable scheme for rewarding the individual. The most striking illustration of this concern over doing justice by the child as a competitive member of society, however, is found in those intricate schemes for weighting credits in terms of the difficulty of the task and the effort put forth by the pupil which have appeared in many schools. In some instances these schemes have even provided for the giving of school credits for washing dishes at home, milking the cows, or playing the piano.

Against this system of artificial rewards and punishments administered in the name of recognizing individual achievement educational theorists and reformers have hammered in vain. In recent years, moreover, it has received support and almost a scientific sanction from the measurement movement. The numerous measurement devices which have been evolved with such feverish haste have tended to give to marks and credits the authority of objectivity and reliability. Also, through the use of speed tests, the stop watch, and the normal probability curve the development of the competitive impulses has been stimulated. The application of the normal curve to the problem of marking is an excellent case in point. After discovering that human abilities tend to distribute themselves in symmetrical fashion about a mode and after discovering further that the older methods of testing and marking are unreliable, certain educational statisticians have suggested that, during the interval which must elapse before the development of objective tests for the measurement of all forms of learning which take place in the school, the pretense of giving to children absolute measures of their achievements be abandoned and a relative marking scale be adopted. This scale, according to a common suggestion, should consist of five steps, and marks should be distributed over the scale in accordance with the expected normal distribution. Thus five per cent., let us say, should receive the first or highest mark, twenty-five per cent. the second, forty per cent. the third, twenty-five per cent. the fourth, and five per cent. the fifth. But the most significant element in the proposal is that each individual should merely be assigned a rank in the group. This practice of course represents a very extreme expression of the general tendency in American education to encourage the individual to regard his own interest as opposed to that of his fellows.

Stimulation of the Competitive Impulses

Much of what has already been said shows that in numerous ways the American school, like American society, stimulates the competitive rather than the collective impulses. It remains only to point out that the general atmosphere of the institution works in the same direction. Consider, for example, the situation as it presents itself in the field of those extra-curriculum activities which have grown up so luxuriantly about secondary

school and college during the last generation—
a vast array of activities including athletics, fraternities, clubs, debating societies, dramatic organizations, and a host of other interests. Of these the
most typical and influential are the athletic activities. Under conditions of most intense competition
individuals are selected to represent the school in
highly spirited contests between institutions. To be
sure, since in many sports the team rather than
the individual is the unit, this process has collec-
tivistic phases; yet the extraordinary attention paid
to outstanding athletes by the school, the community, and the press would seem to exalt again
the principle of individual success. Thus on the
playground, as well as in the classroom, competition for honors among pupils and students appears
to be the driving force.

While deploring certain excesses to which this
competition leads, the American people generally
defend it. As we have seen, they view life itself
in competitive terms and think that the major
function of government is to insure free competition among individuals, organizations, and institutions. In thus exalting the principle of competition
they commonly argue from human nature. They
often say that, if man were only made differently,
education and society might be erected upon differ-

ent foundations. But with man as he is, according to their understanding, high accomplishment in any field must spring from the egoistic rather than the social impulses. They even contend that the social tendencies are effective only because they stimulate individuals to compete for the favors of society. And in support of their argument they always point sooner or later to their own vitality and their genuinely extraordinary achievements in the building of a nation which in their opinion stands as a living monument to individual enterprise.

CHAPTER VI

DEMOCRATIC TRADITION

FOR generations America has been regarded throughout the world as the scene of a gigantic experiment in democracy. While attention has generally been directed primarily towards the political aspect of this experiment, it was much more than a departure from the political forms of the Old World. Fundamentally it was an experiment with a new system of human relationships and a new conception of human worth. Under the conditions which produced the individualism referred to in the preceding chapter there developed a strong faith in the common man and a genuine hatred for those artificial social distinctions which in most societies have divided man from man. An abundance of free land gave to the individual an extraordinary measure of freedom and made impossible for a time and in many regions the erection of a social barrier between employer and employed. The consequence was an equality in social relationships which tends to survive to-day in an altogether different order of society. The

Americans have always deeply resented all claims to social superiority derived from either distinguished ancestry or favored economic position. And it is this willingness on the part of the individual to mingle freely and simply with his neighbors, rather than any abstract theory of social arrangements, which they regard as the essence of democracy.

The principle of democracy has of course exercised a most profound effect on the American system of education. Indeed the more pleasing features of that system may be traced very largely to the influence of the democratic theory and way of life. Thus in its political expression democracy no doubt had much to do with the establishment of free schools. Obviously a government which presumes to rest upon universal suffrage must make provision for the political enlightenment of the masses. Considerations of democracy likewise played an important rôle in the development of the educational ladder. And the program of instruction throughout the educational system seeks to instil the ideals of democracy into the minds of the coming generation. Although the content which has been put into these concepts has commonly been very meager and often misleading, democracy has been a word to conjure with in

America for more than a hundred years. Consequently, when in 1917 President Wilson led the American nation into the World War "to make the world safe for democracy" the people followed him willingly, uncritically, and with enthusiasm.

The Single System

The most magnificent educational product of the American principle of democracy is the *single* educational system. Except for the qualifications to be noted later, the dual system developed in Europe, with its abbreviated program for the masses and its rich offering for the classes, has never existed in the United States. Thus, the American system of schools constitutes not only an educational ladder, but a *single* educational ladder. This sequential organization of institutions, consisting of primary, secondary, and higher schools, is theoretically open to all elements in the population and is commonly looked upon by the Americans themselves as their system of education. The exceptions which exist are usually brushed aside as unimportant and irrelevant.

According to the theory of education most frequently expounded in America the public school should have no competitor. Into its classrooms and shops and playgrounds should come all the children of all the people. Here, under the supervision of democratically minded teachers, these children from all social groups and from all stations in life should work and play together. The more gifted, regardless of parental status, should be encouraged to proceed to the higher schools and universities and there be equipped for positions of leadership in the economic, political, and intellectual life of the nation; the remainder should leave school near the close of the secondary period to perform the more simple tasks of society. In this way the biological resources of the entire population would be rationally utilized, and the school would be made to promote the reconciliation of social groups and classes. Although this statement represents an ideal formulation of the theory, in many American communities it is in close harmony with the facts. There are, however, several important points at which practice parts company with theory.

It is not strictly true to say that America has a *single* system of education. In addition to the public schools there are numerous private schools in the United States. Certain of these institutions, such as those which are organized and supported by religious sects, may be disregarded in this connection because the tuition charges are low and the pupils are consequently fairly representative of the population. Thus the Catholic schools, for example, are very much like the public schools in the social composition of their pupils. Many of the great universities likewise, though supported out of private funds, are essentially public institutions. But there are in America certain schools—primary, secondary, and higher—which charge heavy tuition fees, which cater definitely to favored families, and which may be regarded fundamentally as class institutions. Some of these schools strive in various subtle ways to attract children from homes of great wealth or social distinction. Thus, the imposing register of the names of the students, which is often prominently displayed in the catalogues, is obviously calculated to impress the prospective patron with the aristocratic tone of the school.

Perhaps the most striking instance, however, of an approach to a dual system of education is found in the former slave states of the south. In these states, of which there are fifteen besides the District of Columbia, two parallel systems of schools are maintained—the one for whites and the other for negroes. As a general rule the schools for the colored race have been very inadequately supported and have been confined largely to the primary level. Although more ample provision is now being made for the education of negroes, there is little likelihood that the partiality towards the favored race will disappear or even be radically moderated in the immediate future. Under a comple equalization of conditions, however, the dual system would remain and with it the denial of the democratic principle in its application to the negro.

In this connection a word should be said about other forms of racial discrimination as they affect the extension of educational opportunity. The negro, though the object of the greatest antipathy and injustice, does not suffer alone. There is in America a prejudice on the part of the older inhabitants who come from the north and west of Europe against the newer stocks from the south and east. Along the Pacific coast there is an even stronger prejudice against the orientals and particularly the Japanese. The way in which these prejudices may operate is well illustrated in the case of the Jews who are very numerous in the great industrial cities. In many private schools, even schools which are styled progressive, the attendance of Jews is limited to a certain percentage of the enrollment. And quite recently the oldest and most powerful university in the country discussed publicly the question of adopting the principle of limitation. Fortunately, discrimination of this type has thus far been confined to private schools; but the practice of drawing the boundary lines of districts in such a way as to confine certain races to particular schools is by no means unknown in American cities.

Yet one additional fact marring the theory of the single system should be observed. Differences in wealth and family tradition in America are colossal; and these differences have a marked effect upon the extension of educational opportunity. It is of course beyond the period of compulsory education in particular that these forces operate most effectually. Although the public high school has expanded at an extraordinary rate during the past generation, it enrolls to-day only about one-half of the children of appropriate age. In the college and the university the proportion of the population in attendance is naturally much further reduced. This gradual elimination of students from the upper levels of the system is apparently due in considerable measure to family circumstance. As a consequence, many individuals of superior natural gifts are practically denied advanced educational opportunities, and the positions of leadership in society, in so far as they are dependent on schooling, fall in disproportionate numbers to members of the more favored classes. The thesis can easily be defended, however, that up to the present time the American system of public education has come nearer than any other to the ideal of equalizing educational opportunity.

The Comprehensive Secondary School

The principle of democracy has received one of its most interesting applications in the organization of the public high school. During the early part of the present century, when the program of secondary education was expanding, the introduction of the more practical subjects pointing directly to the vocations precipitated a vigorous controversy regarding the form that the high school should take. Some argued in the name of efficiency that the different interests should be housed in different buildings and be provided with different managements; others argued in the name of democracy that all of these interests should be brought together in one institution. According to the first proposal the secondary school system of a large city would include a series of specialized schools, while according to the second it would consist of but a single type of comprehensive school organized in sufficient numbers to meet the demand for adolescent education. Although both plans have found expression in America, the second is the more popular and seems to have triumphed. The typical secondary school in the United States is consequently an institution which embraces within its program the entire range of subjects from auto-mechanics to Latin and from painting to trigonometry. It also enrolls among its pupils children with the most diverse cultural backgrounds and the most varied vocational interests.

Many factors, of course, have operated to bring about the triumph of the comprehensive school, but the argument that it represents the more democratic solution of the problem has had large theoretical influence. According to this argument, which throws a clear light on the American conception of democracy, the organization of separate institutions for the teaching of the industrial arts, the commercial branches, and the older academic subjects would divide the adolescent population into distinct occupational groups and thus tend to recognize and accentuate the differences which already exist in adult society. On the other hand, the establishment of the comprehensive high school would bring all children together, regardless of their occupational futures, and thus prolong into the period of adolescence the common associations provided by the public elementary school.

Here again it appears that the Americans are less anxious to remove social and economic inequalities than to obscure the existence and moderate the effects of such inequalities. Indeed they are generally inclined to deny that classes exist in their society. In support of this contention they point to the relative absence of the rigid social stratification of the Old World and the comparative ease with which individuals of talent and ambition overcome social barriers and achieve eminence in finance, industry, and government. Thus, to them democracy resides essentially in a condition of social mobility and the willingness of all groups to live together without bitterness or hatred. In realizing this conception of democracy they believe that the comprehensive school will render valuable service.

Social Relationships Among Pupils

The relationships which prevail among pupils in the American public school are on the whole democratic and free. This is particularly true at the elementary school level before children have become conscious of the inequalities of the adult world. But even in the secondary school and the university, provided the student has sufficient means to maintain the ordinary standards of dress set by the more prosperous classes, he is not greatly handicapped in his relations with his fellows by obscure origins and modest family connections. He is judged very largely on the basis of his own personal qualities. And if he is especially gifted in those directions which command the interest and respect of his classmates, particularly if he is proficient in athletics or in some other student activity, the fact that he comes from a poor or uncultured home may increase his prestige. The circumstance may even attract the attention of the press and be made the subject of an editorial on the equality of opportunity in America.

Another line of evidence bearing upon this question which merits attention is the widespread practice among students of working their way through secondary school and college. One-half or even three-fourths of the young men in one of these institutions may devote a goodly portion of their leisure hours to some form of remunerative labor. For a student thus to meet all of the expenses which attendance at high school or college entails is by no means rare. Because of the somewhat different economic position of woman in the traditional order, girls earn their way much less frequently than boys, but even among them the custom is not uncommon.

The forms of labor in which a student may engage are most diverse—nothing from tending furnaces to tutoring in languages is barred. The only requisite is that the work be well-paid. The fact of major interest, however, is that very little, if any, social stigma attaches to the practice. Participation in even the roughest type of manual labor, though entirely beneath the dignity of a university graduate except as an avocation, will be extenuated in a student on the grounds that "he is working his way through college" and is consequently headed for an occupation of unquestioned respectability.

Certain tendencies are appearing in the school, however, which seriously mar the democracy of the social relationships among the pupils. Racial prejudices and antipathies very early penetrate the school from the outside. Representatives from the less favored races and nationalities are often forced to accept an inferior social status. They may even be denied membership in various clubs and societies organized by the pupils.

A yet more flagrant denial of the American principle of democracy is found in the social fraternity which during the last one hundred years has spread through the colleges and even reached the high schools. This organization is commonly national in scope and embraces numerous chapters or locals in different educational institutions of a given type or grade. The members of each chapter constitute a self-governing body and extend invitations of membership to selected individuals among the students. These selections are entirely in the hands of the organization and are generally made on the basis of a number of factors, such as family prestige, wealth of parents, leadership in student activities, and general good fellowship. Although scholarship is often taken into account, the emphasis is placed rather on the more strictly personal considerations. Fraternities are thus essentially undemocratic institutions and tend to introduce into the school an element of social snobbishness. The American people have recognized this in many states by passing laws prohibiting their establishment in public secondary schools. At the college level, however, little effort has been made to curb them, partly because they had become deeply entrenched and powerful before the public discovered them and partly because the college is somewhat remote from the people and dominated to a considerable degree by an aristocratic tradition.

Social Relationships Between Teacher and Pupil

From kindergarten to graduate school the social relationships between teacher and pupil are free and informal. To be sure, the old tradition that the teacher is a monarch in his little domain still prevails to some extent, and he often takes advantage of the authority of his position. Nevertheless even in the university the teacher is extremely approachable. A professor of world renown will meet his students on a plane of equality, discuss their problems with them, and invite them to his home. The American teacher has created but few of those artificial barriers which in so many parts of the world serve to separate the teacher from his pupils. The result may be a somewhat extravagant dissipation of his energies, but this loss is more than offset by the naturalness of the relationship developed and the consequent enlargement of the teacher's influence over the pupil. It also increases the intimacy of the contact between the school and social life.

During the past generation many efforts have been made further to democratize the teacher-pupil relationship and to make the pupil a more active participant in the various activities of the school. Even where a delightful condition of informality between teacher and pupil prevails, the attitude of the teacher is very often the attitude of the benevolent autocrat. The project method, the socialized recitation, pupil government, and the progressive education movement all represent a general interest in drawing the pupil actively into the whole educative process and thus making the school a genuinely democratic institution. These movements, however, though perhaps still in their early stages, have been less successful than was anticipated in changing the character of the public school. This has been due in part no doubt to the tremendous inertia of a vast system of education. But perhaps of more significance is the genuine opposition encountered in certain quarters. As we shall point out in a later section of this volume, there are at work in American education and social life various forces of mechanization which have little in common with the democratic principle. At present these forces tend to triumph in both school and society.

Social Relationships Among Teachers

The principle of democracy has also penetrated to a considerable degree into the relationships which exist among teachers. This perhaps is best exemplified by the great educational conventions which occur twice every year. At these nation-wide meetings will be found teachers and administrators from every level of the educational system. While those working in particular types of institutions or those with particular interests have their separate organizations and arrange programs which deal with their special problems, provision is made for general meetings at which the most diverse points of view are presented by representatives from different parts of the system. On the same program may appear a kindergarten teacher, an elementary school principal, a high school instructor, a university professor, a superintendent of schools, and a president of a great university. And both in the regular meetings and at numerous informal gatherings workers from all divisions of the educational enterprise mingle in the freest possible fashion. They seem to feel themselves members of the same great fellowship. This is all in harmony with the theory of democracy which is generally accepted in America to-day.

At certain points, however, where, as the Americans think, they are still influenced by traditions and practices borrowed from beyond the Atlantic, the democracy within the profession is incomplete.

The notion still prevails that the social position of a secondary school teacher is superior to that of the teacher of little children, and that the social position of the college or university professor is superior to both. Moreover, the teachers of the older and more aristocratic disciplines in the higher institutions tend to regard themselves as a little better than the teachers of the newer subjects. Yet it should be said that these differences in prestige are traceable very largely to differences in training and compensation. Thus, in the past elementary teachers have commonly been given an abbreviated and narrow training in normal schools, while secondary teachers have enjoyed the richer cultural opportunities of the colleges and the universities. But with the rise of teachers colleges and the development of university departments devoted to the study of the problems of the lower schools, these differences are tending to disappear. Many communities also are adopting what is called a single salary schedule for elementary and secondary teachers. Under this arrangement the position of the teacher in the system has no bearing on compensation: the only factors taken into account are training, experience, and ability. To the extent that these changes become general the relationships among teachers will assume a yet more democratic character.

There is another point also at which this democracy within the profession is defective. In spite of the enormous gains made by women in America during the last one hundred years in their efforts to win opportunity in the spheres of industry, government, and education, they still suffer from grievous handicaps and injustices. And nowhere are the difficulties under which they labor more clearly shown than in the field of teaching. Although two-thirds of the teachers in the secondary school and practically all of the teachers in the elementary school are women, the overwhelming majority of the professorships in the universities and the important administrative positions throughout the educational system fall to men. Moreover, for the same type of work a woman is commonly paid less than a man. There is also a curious and widespread discrimination against the employment of married women in the schools. In many systems a woman teacher on getting married is expected to relinquish her position. While this may be due in part to a feeling that a woman who has other means of support should not be permitted to compete with her less fortunate sisters, it is undoubtedly traceable very largely to the conviction that the place of the married woman is in the home. Since the sex code as it applies to women is quite severe and probably quite rigorously followed, the early schooling of children is placed almost altogether in the hands of women who lack the experiences of both sex and motherhood. The relation of this question to the processes of education and the rights of women are rarely considered by American educators.

Coeducation of the Sexes

America is the classical land of the coeducation of the sexes. Within the limits of the system of public education boys and girls, men and women, usually attend the same institutions. To this generalization there are of course some important exceptions. In the larger population centers of the south and east the two sexes are often segregated at the secondary school level, and occasionally in the colleges and universities. In the private schools in these same areas and at all levels of the system separation is not only common but seems to be the rule. When full allowance, however, is made for these exceptions the fact remains that the overwhelming majority of the schools of America are attended by both sexes.

Educational theorists in the United States are almost unanimously in favor of coeducation. The arguments which they advance are well-known. They maintain that when boys and girls are permitted to grow up together both sexes develop more normally, the danger of sex perversion is moderated, and a sounder basis is laid for marriage and family life. They also say that under the conditions of coeducation each sex exercises a salutary influence over the other—the boy stimulating the girl to a more active and vigorous life and the girl exerting a refining and softening influence over the boy. They argue further that daily association tends to substitute for the purely sexual attraction a general feeling of comradeship. Although to all of these claims some dissenting voices are raised and from time to time the charge is made that gross immorality is rampant in the high schools and colleges attended by both sexes, the American people seem to be definitely committed to both the theory and the practice of coeducation.

Coeducation in the United States, however, was not a product of theoretical analysis. Like the American system of education in general it simply grew out of the conditions of life. It represents essentially a democratic and popular response to the problem of providing boys and girls with the opportunities of schooling. Among the masses, where both men and women must work and share more or less equally the economic burdens of existence, the thought of segregating the two sexes at school is not likely to arise; and if it does arise, it is not likely to be given serious consideration. Ordinary persons are harassed so perpetually by the stern demands of life that questions of sex are forced into a secondary position. Preoccupation with sex is a product of leisure and is therefore commonly confined to those classes whose members are freed from the necessity of devoting their energies to grappling with the problems of food, clothing, and shelter. It is therefore no accident that the separation of boys and girls is found chiefly in the private schools which cater to the favored classes and in the public schools of the more conservative regions of the east and south; that in certain southern cities the two sexes are segregated in the schools for white children and taught together in the schools for negroes; that the first American college open equally to men and women was founded in 1833 in the frontier state of Ohio; or that the country west of the Alleghenies, the land of the pioneer and the common man, remains to-day the stronghold of coeducation.

In conclusion the limitations of the conception
of coeducation which prevails in the United States
should be indicated. The Americans regard coeducation as involving nothing more than the simul-
taneous attendance of both sexes at the same
educational institution. This conception is therefore entirely compatible with the use of the school
to prepare boys and girls for quite different rôles
in the economic and social order. The organization
of separate programs of instruction for the two
sexes in high school and college is consequently
not surprising. While there are many common
elements in these programs, the school nevertheless tends to identify woman with the home and
the more sedentary occupations and to associate
man with shop, field, and factory. Although
powerful social forces are rapidly breaking down
the barriers which in the past have kept the sexes
in two fairly distinct spheres, the school for the
most part accepts the traditional order and serves
as a conservative influence in society. And in this
respect, as well as in others, the conception of
democracy which the school seeks to enforce is
the conception which is embodied in the mores of
the American people.

CHAPTER VII

NATIONAL SOLIDARITY

THROUGHOUT a very large part of their history the American people have manifested a deep concern over the question of social solidarity. This is due to the fact that, except for brief periods during recent generations, they have felt themselves either the victims of insecurity or the champions of a great cause. In either case the necessity of promoting group solidarity has seemed urgent. Although the sentiment of nationality was practically absent during the colonial era, because the various settlements had been founded under different auspices and were widely separated in space and also because they all felt a genuine allegiance to the countries from which they had sprung and looked to the Old World for both cultural and political leadership, nevertheless the need for social cohesion was keenly felt. The conditions which have fostered this perennial interest in some form of solidarity may be found in the hazards which surrounded the early colonists, the various wars which the American people have fought, and the feeling of a cultural mission which has always dominated their mentality.

Conditions Fostering Concern over Solidarity

During the period of colonization in the seventeenth and eighteenth centuries the European settlers along the Atlantic coast were very conscious of the fact that they were living in a strange country separated from the homeland by thousands of miles of ocean. They also knew only too well that they were surrounded by Indian tribes whose hostility might take an active form at any moment. In the grim struggle for existence which was thus thrust upon them they soon learned by bitter experience that life itself was the price which they would have to pay for the failure of the individual to subordinate himself to the welfare of the group. Under these conditions of physical and material insecurity, which followed the advancing frontier to the Pacific and prevailed in some parts of the United States until well towards the close of the nineteenth century, there was a natural and inevitable demand for social solidarity.

Although the American people have always professed a great love of peace, they have nevertheless fought many wars. During the colonial period, besides waging numerous battles with the Indians on their own account, they were of course ranged by the side of the mother country in all of the conflicts in which she found herself engaged. And no sooner had conditions of life become fairly stable and secure east of the Alleghenies than thirteen of the English colonies in North America in 1776 rebelled against the authority of London and precipitated a struggle for independence which culminated in the founding of the nation. A generation later the young republic fought a second war with England, and in 1845 pursued a policy of conquest in the southwest by engaging in a brief struggle with the neighboring state of Mexico. Then in the sixties the country was ravaged for five years by a bitter civil strife between the North and the South. Arising out of sectional differences generated by economic rivalry and a controversy over the institution of human slavery, this internecine quarrel almost destroyed the Union and released passions so intense that they survive even to this day. Thereafter followed another period of peace which was marked by a slow economic recuperation in the South and an extraordinary industrial expansion in the North and West. But in 1898 the country again resorted to the sword, closed the colonial career of Spain, and herself ventured upon the path of imperialism. Finally, in 1917 America entered the World War in the name of democracy and in 1918 emerged as the first power of the world and a conservative nation. Since the successful prosecution of war by a political democracy depends to a peculiar degree upon popular support, these military enterprises have aroused in the American people from generation to generation an ever-recurring interest in national solidarity.

More important, however, than the hazards of frontier life or the military struggles of the nation was the tradition of a revolutionary mission which the American people fostered for generations. When the young republic first took its place among the nations of the world it stood in the very forefront of time and championed a set of revolutionary principles which threatened with dissolution the existing forms of government. It exalted the rights of ordinary men, glorified the virtues of democracy, and challenged the authority of monarchs. Little wonder therefore that its representatives often received frigid welcomes in the capitals of Europe and that its citizens generally felt themselves to be dwelling in a hostile world. Existence itself must have seemed precarious to this little nation living on the borders of civilization and embracing three million inhabitants widely scattered through the American wilderness. Without wealth, without trained armies, without cultural tradition, and without experience in national government it faced the future. Even its friends in other parts of the world doubted that it could endure, and its enemies prophesied its speedy collapse. The American people consequently felt that their institutions were constantly in danger and that they should be prepared at any moment to present a united front towards the reactionary forces of the Old World. At the same time they were supremely convinced that they marched in the vanguard of progress and that their experiment should be defended not only in their own interests but also in the interests of all the peoples of the earth.

Although in the course of the nineteenth century both the domestic and the world situations changed radically, this view prevailed generally in the United States down to the days of the October Revolution in Russia in 1917. In the spring of that year the American people had entered the war against the Central Powers in the firm belief that they were carrying on the revolutionary tradition and were crusading for the ideals of democracy, but before peace was concluded they were concerned less over the fate of monarchy than over the spread of Bolshevism. As the full import of the nature of the new doctrine was grasped, many whose ancestors had rejoiced to make kings tremble on their thrones saw far less of menace in the pomp of the Kaiser than in the teachings of Lenin. Thus, after a century and a half of radicalism they found themselves in the ranks of the conservatives; and a people that for generations had welcomed and even fostered revolutions in all parts of the world now began to fear the very word revolution. But the need for solidarity in a world which to them appeared to be drifting toward chaos seemed just as necessary as it ever had in the early days of the republic. To-day, although they have recovered from their first fright, they are in no mood to lend encouragement to any form of radical teachings in economics and politics.

Intolerance of Cultural and Racial Diversity

At the root of the American theory of society is the settled conviction that an essentially homogeneous people is the only solid foundation upon which to erect a political state. They believe that heterogeneity of either race or culture is certain to lead to separatist political tendencies which in turn will lead inevitably to conflict and federal disintegration. They even seem to regard the ties of a common origin, a common language, and a common historical tradition as stronger than economic interest. Since the founding of the Union they have consequently tended to question the patriotism of those elements differing appreciably in race, speech, or religion from the *original stock* which was recruited almost altogether from the non-Catholic population of the British Isles. Prior to the last generation, however, and particularly before the Russian Revolution, this opposition to racially and culturally diverse elements was tempered somewhat by a general feeling of sympathy for the oppressed of all countries. During at least the earlier part of her history America was rightly regarded by the masses everywhere as a land of promise and by dissentient spirits throughout the world as a haven of refuge. Nevertheless even from the first the thought has persisted that the nation can shelter but one culture and that all newcomers should become Americanized.

The situation in the United States with respect to peoples and cultures is of course radically unlike that faced in the older countries of the world. At the beginning of the nineteenth century America was a land of unsurpassed natural resources and at the same time practically uninhabited. Consequently, as soon as the development of transportation and communication provided the means, a gigantic stream of immigration began to pour into the country. First it came from the British Isles, later from Germany and Scandinavia, then from the south and east of Europe, and finally even from the teeming populations of Asia. The original response on the part of the American people ranged all the way from indifference to cordial welcome. But as economic conditions changed, as the political temper of the nation cooled, as less assimilable stocks began to arrive, and as evidence accumulated that certain groups resist Americanization, the attitude gradually altered and a spirit of opposition to immigration spread through the country. This reversal of feeling culminated in 1924 in the passage by the federal congress of a drastic and thoroughgoing restrictive act.

Since the American people identify nationality with culture, they have insisted that these newcomers should become like themselves in dress, language, and habit of thought as quickly as possible. With the exception of a handful of dreamers, they consequently take no interest whatsoever in any theoretical discussion about making American soil the scene of an idealistic experiment in the political integration of a variety of cultural forms. They are rather inclined to point to Europe and to conclude that her long history of strife is the natural fruit of differences in language and ideal. Moreover, they confidently believe that their own country enjoys a special dispensation from Providence, that their civilization is superior to all others, and that their institutions are certain to spread over the earth. Being honestly incapable therefore of understanding why any immigrant group should desire to cling to its own culture, they have at all times, and more particularly during periods of crisis, sought to make "good Americans" of all who came to their shores. The degree to which they have succeeded in this aim is truly remarkable and a source of great pride to them. In this process of welding the most diverse elements into a single nation the public school has no doubt played a large rôle.

Compulsory Education

The fundamental instrument which the Americans have fashioned for the promotion of national solidarity is compulsory education. Beginning with the enactment of a part-time compulsory-attendance law in Massachusetts in 1852 the movement designed to bring the entire child population under the influence of the school has now spread to all the states of the Union. Owing to the fact that, according to the American custom, each state enjoys practical autonomy in the field of education, the laws passed by the different commonwealths vary greatly in their provisions. There is, however, a general tendency to require all children to attend school during the period of elementary education or between the ages of six or seven and fourteen years. Within the last decade various states have broken with this precedent of thinking of compulsory education exclusively in terms of childhood and have enacted legislation which requires either part- or full-time attendance at school to the age of eighteen. Thus, the proposal that secondary education be made universal is being given serious consideration in the United States to-day. Apparently the American people are definitely committed to the doctrine of education by compulsion.

The theory underlying this doctrine is not altogether simple. In passing their compulsory education laws the Americans have been moved by a variety of considerations. No doubt they have taken this step partly because they wish to protect the child from exploitation by ignorant or vicious parents, partly because they feel impelled to provide suitable occupation for children made idle by child labor laws, partly because they have come to regard some measure of schooling in the nature of an individual right, partly because they possess a mystical faith in the power and general beneficence of "education," and partly because they believe that the stability of a political democracy must rest upon the intelligence of its citizens. But perhaps an even more compelling motive has been their concern over national solidarity. The vastness of the country, the ethnic heterogeneity of the population, and the relative weakness of social tradition have all combined to make imperative the fashioning of some artificial means of creating a common social mind throughout the nation. Results which in older civilizations and more compact populations may be expected to flow naturally out of the life of the community, the American people have sought to achieve through the school.

The Basic Common Education

Under the traditional system of education, which still generally prevails in America, the elementary school embraces eight years of instruction. The fact that in some parts of the country the program of this institution has been seven and in some parts nine years in length may be disregarded. Whatever the scope of the program, the obvious intent of the earlier compulsory education laws was to establish the principle that all children should finish the elementary school. And the curriculum of this institution is undifferentiated in its content. For the most part, all children pursue the same subjects and participate in the same activities. Provision for individual differences is made, not by altering the materials of the program, but by permitting children to progress at different rates. To this statement many exceptions may be found in the more progressive centers, but it constitutes a fairly accurate generalization for the rank and file of public elementary schools.

The basic common education is often justified on the grounds that it provides for the acquisition of those attitudes, skills, and knowledges which every individual must possess in order to meet the ordinary social situations and to perform the unspecialized activities of life. This thought no doubt enters into the theory, but certainly of equal importance to the American people is the consideration that the solidarity of the nation must rest upon a foundation of common ideas, beliefs, sentiments, and loyalties. In the absence of such a common body of experience they feel that collective action would be impossible and that the safety of the republic would be endangered. An examination of the content of the program lends weight to this interpretation. The curriculum of the elementary school abounds with materials drawn from the history of the American people and is confined almost entirely to the native culture.

How important the Americans regard this basic common education was revealed a few years ago when the movement for the general reorganization of their system of education was being initiated. Among other things the movement called for the downward extension of the secondary school to embrace the last two years of the traditional elementary school. Although the object of this particular reform was the creation of a junior high school with a program far richer than the curriculum for the same years under the conventional arrangement, the theoretical opposition was not silenced until it was thoroughly convinced that the new institution would reduce neither the amount nor the quality of this common education. The argument was advanced with particular force that the coming of industrial civilization with its numerous differentiations and divisions gave reason for extending rather than for reducing the integrating power of the school. And to-day there is much evidence to indicate that the common elements in the secondary school curriculum of the future will be considerably increased.

Emphasis on Civic Training

In recent years the problem of civic education has aroused much interest in the United States. Almost since the opening of the present century the question has received particularly widespread attention. It has been discussed in both the professional and the general press, it has been studied by numerous local and national committees of teachers, it has been given a place on the programs of various organizations of laymen, and it has been made the object of serious scientific investigation. At the present time a powerful committee, amply supplied with funds and widely representative of American education and science, is launching a five-year program of inquiry into every phase of the teaching of the social studies. Moreover, new courses in government, civics, sociology, economics, history and ethics without number have already been introduced into the schools; and experiments in pupil government have been given trial in hundreds of places. Apparently the American people are deadly in earnest about becoming better citizens, or at least about making better citizens of their children.

In this concern over training for citizenship there seem to be two opposing views among the educational theorists. On the one side are the conservatives who are becoming greatly alarmed at the evidence of the decay of the ancestral order which they see accumulating on every hand. They point to the increase of crime, the loss of interest in politics, the rapid rise in the divorce rate, the growing disrespect for law, the declining prestige of the church, the relaxing of the moral code, the spread of skeptical doctrines, and the general weakening of all traditional creeds and faiths. They are inclined to trace many of these phenomena to the coming of "soft pedagogy" in educational theory and to the tendency to follow the interest of the pupil in educational practice. Their remedy is therefore simple. They would restore the principle of discipline to its historical place in the school, introduce a little "iron" into the methods of instruction, and teach children their duties in the social order.

With both the diagnosis and the remedy of the conservatives the radicals are in disagreement. They argue that the phenomena which cause so much alarm are by no means due to changes in ed-

ucational methods but are rather the product of
new modes of life ushered in by the machine age.
They contend that industrialism is rapidly destroying those social forces which preserved order and
enforced the will of the group in the simple agrarian society of the past. Their solution, however,
in so far as they have one, is fundamentally intellectual. They are confident that there must be
a general reconstruction of society, but they have
no positive social program to propose. They would
merely use the school as an instrument for making the coming generation intelligent about this
new industrial civilization and its problems. Their
hope is that the citizens of the future will thus be
equipped to bear their particular civic burdens in
the way that seems best to them, and that they
will impose upon themselves whatever of discipline the conditions of life may make necessary.
This doctrine of course represents a repudiation
of the principle of social solidarity, but there seems
to be little likelihood that it will ever gain wide
popular support.

The Cult of Patriotism

In this battle of the theorists the American people as a whole seem to be but little interested. In

so far as they take sides they are naturally inclined more towards the conservative than towards the radical view; but when they think of good citizenship they think primarily of patriotism and civic loyalty. They are convinced that, if the citizen is sufficiently patriotic, he will behave as he should behave in all social situations. Patriotism, however, is seldom defined further than to embrace a knowledge of the federal constitution, an unenlightened veneration of the founders of the republic, and a willingness to die for one's country. Although such a conception of patriotism may appear to lack imagination, it prevails in most countries and tends to shape the program of civic education everywhere. In America, moreover, as in other lands, it assumes its more extreme and irrational forms in times of great national stress. Thus, during the period of the Great War and the years immediately following, the public school in the United States became a powerful engine of patriotism, spread military propaganda among the masses, and served generally to promote an intense form of national solidarity.

In the teaching of patriotism the Americans employ various devices in their schools. The reading materials of the elementary school are often nationalistic in tone, and the study of American history and civilization is emphasized at both the primary and secondary levels. In the past the history textbooks employed have given much space to the various wars waged by the United States; and even to-day the military element, though somewhat reduced, receives much attention. Moreover, in spite of the efforts of historians to reform the teaching of history and to bring it into closer harmony with the facts, the pupil gains the impression from the textbook that his country has never waged an unjust war, that the motives of its statesmen have always been above criticism, and that in its relations with other nations it has ever been inspired by ideals of righteousness and fair dealing. He also is led to conclude that the American soldier is probably without an equal in the world and that military enterprise provides the most heroic service which a citizen can render his country. The founding fathers likewise receive a strongly biased treatment in the schools. They are made to appear as men of gigantic stature and of almost superhuman wisdom. Their handiwork, the federal constitution, consequently carries an authority which places it beyond the reach of the present generation of men. The saluting of the flag and other forms designed to arouse national loyalties are also practiced in many schools. Thus everywhere public education is regarded as an instrument for the teaching of patriotism; and this teaching, in so far as it has not been deliberately organized for the protection of vested and selfish interests, has aimed primarily at the promotion of national solidarity. The emphasis, however, since attention is focused primarily on past achievements and since the conditions of life have changed radically in recent generations, is essentially conservative in tone.

CHAPTER VIII

SOCIAL CONFORMITY

THE American interest in group solidarity may at first appear to be subsumed under the broader principle of social conformity. Although this relationship may exist at certain times and places, it is not a necessary relationship. Thus group solidarity may be exacted for the purpose of propagating some radical political ideal or of promoting some vast program of social reconstruction. The former seems to have provided the inspiration for that solidarity which characterized the American people during the early days of the republic, while the latter appears to be the driving force behind the solidarity which features life in Soviet Russia to-day. However, since the interest in solidarity in the United States has lost its earlier ideal content and has become essentially conservative, in its present form it may therefore be regarded as a phase of the general American concern over social conformity.

It should of course not be assumed that the American people are conformists in all directions.

Indeed in certain spheres they have always placed a premium upon initiative and creative endeavor. Thus in the realm of industrial technique they perhaps surpass all other peoples in their readiness to discard old and adopt new devices and processes. In fact they spend enormous sums of money every year in the conscious and directed search for mechanical improvements, and in this world of practical affairs they never show the slightest desire to cling to anything merely because it was used by their grandfathers. Here they even seem to be predisposed to doubt the utility of any tool or procedure hallowed with age.

In the wide areas of politics, economics, morals, and religion, however, they exhibit a decidedly different mentality. In these departments of experience they seem to place no premium whatsoever upon invention and originality; rather do they seek to discourage bold speculation and radical experimentation of every kind. Thus, while they regard the application of thought to industrial processes as highly desirable and beneficent, they tend to view searching inquiry into the sphere of social and human relations as fraught with great danger. Although, since the coming of the Puritans, there has been a powerful conformist strain in American life, this concern over conformity has not always been as strong or as widely prevalent as it is to-day. At one time, as the entire world knows, America was a land of new experiments in politics and economics; and in the nineteenth century she bore a numerous progeny of sects, cults, and movements in the field of religion and morals. Moreover, she extended the hospitality of her shores to dissenting persons and groups from all over the world. The extent of the contrast between the old and the new America is found in the fact that to-day a prospective citizen seeking admission must first submit to an examination of the ideas which he proposes to bring into the country. And if his ideas are not sound, according to the standards set by conservative forces, he is asked to go elsewhere.

The reader may feel that two of the principles suggested in the present outline, the principle of individual success and the principle of social conformity, are mutually incompatible. Such, however, is not the case. There would no doubt be a complete and irreconcilable conflict between a throughgoing individualism, on the one hand, and an insistence upon social conformity, on the other. But concern over promoting individual success and the organization of society about the principle of individualism are two very different things. In fact the emphasis in America on individual *success*, since society must after all define the goals to be striven for and the standards by which individual performance is to be judged, constitutes a most emphatic denial of genuine individualism. Under such conditions, particularly if such ideals and standards are narrow, as they are in America, the individual must of necessity feel himself driven by hostile social forces and thwarted at a hundred points. Thus, the urge to success may prove to be the most austere and merciless of masters. The Americans, however, because of their pioneering past and their former life of agrarian isolation, are fond of calling themselves individualists and of singing the praises of individualism. Nevertheless the individualistic tradition, except as it finds expression in the narrow sphere of competition for pecuniary success, is out of accord with present-day conditions in America and serves to obscure the real nature of the contemporary social order.

The Standardization of Life

This tendency towards the enforcement of social conformity has been accelerated in certain ways by the coming of industrial civilization. In fact this civilization seems to be providing the instruments for the thorough standardization of life. The development of modern means of transportation and communication, which has gone farther in America than in any other part of the world, has destroyed the isolation of the agrarian order and has closely integrated the various sections of this vast country. The rise of distinct cultures in different parts of the nation is thus rendered extremely difficult and improbable. Their 25,000,000 automobiles alone have given the American people a mobility that is entirely without precedent in history. Moreover, gigantic manufacturing establishments produce standardized goods for nation-wide consumption, and equally gigantic commercial enterprises dispense the same products from one end of the country to the other. Whether it be neckties or sermons, pickles or concerts, baked beans or moving pictures, underwear or sports, automobiles or news articles, silk stockings or poetry, the American people increasingly wear the same clothes, eat the same food, play the same games, see the same sights, discuss the same subjects, listen to the same music, think the same thoughts, and laugh over the same jokes. Apparently industrialism has made possible, and some think inevitable, the fashioning of an entire people after a single pattern.

There is, however, another side to this picture

which should be examined. The new civilization is undoubtedly freeing the individual from the coercive influence of the small family or community group. In the past the individual ordinarily has been compelled to live under the very eyes of his parents and his grandparents and his brothers and his sisters and his cousins and his uncles and his aunts, as well as within the immediate presence of his neighbors and Mrs. Grundy. To-day he may at his pleasure withdraw from this group, lose his identity in the great city, and become a different person. He may in fact choose his companions as he would choose his clothes and thus order a society according to his own tastes. Almost regardless of his ideas on politics, economics, religion, or morals, he can find others of congenial mind and associate himself with them. It is altogether possible therefore that these standardizing tendencies of industrial civilization are superficial and that contrary forces of a more fundamental character are at work. Perhaps the new culture will embrace a wide geographical area and thus appear to produce uniformity, but within this area there may be a complexity, a variety, and a richness of life which was impossible in the small agrarian community. But whatever the future may hold in store, the immediate result in America seems to be widespread standardization of taste and a general regimentation of thought.

Methods of Curriculum-making

The way in which the principle of social conformity finds expression in American education is perhaps best illustrated by the methods of curriculum-making which have come into vogue in recent years. For various reasons that need not be examined here educational leaders have become interested in the general task of selecting and organizing the materials of instruction to be employed in the school. Since this interest in curriculum-making happened to be very intimately associated with the movement for the application of the scientific method to the study of education, there was a natural insistence that the problem be attacked in a scientific manner. As a result the emphasis almost everywhere has been placed on objective and even mechanical methods of analysis and measurement. Of the various procedures suggested the method of social analysis and the method of consensus of opinion have been most widely used.

Both of these methods suffer from the same disability. They both tend to begin and end with the present social situation. According to the method of social analysis, the activities in which people engage in contemporary American life should be objectively studied and the desirable activities which are inadequately or imperfectly performed should receive attention in the school. Investigators who have employed this method, however, have become well aware of its limitations. They have discovered that no amount of purely objective study of life activities will produce standards whereby the good may be distinguished from the bad, or the better from the worse. They have discovered furthermore that this process of evaluation is the very essence of curriculum-making. The way out of the dilemma which they have proposed is to apply to the results of social analysis the method of consensus of opinion. Thus they would approach their most worthy citizens and derive from collective judgments standards for the evaluation of the various activities which might be introduced into the school.

The almost certain outcome under the American social and political system of the application of these methods to curriculum-making is obvious. It is apparent that the crucial point in the procedure is the selection of the judges; and it is equally apparent that with rare exceptions the persons asked to serve in this capacity will be those who have been successful according to the standards inherent in American civilization. Moreover, in passing judgment upon the tasks of the school they will undoubtedly for the most part give expression to these standards. The inevitable consequence is that the school will become an instrument for the perpetuation of the existing social order rather than a creative force in society.

This attack on the curriculum has revealed a fundamental and irreconcilable difference of opinion among American educational theorists. On the one side are ranged those who believe that the function of the school is essentially conservative, and on the other those who like to think of the school as an agency of social reconstruction. At present the first theory is supported, either consciously or unwittingly, by the great body of practical people, teachers as well as laymen, while the second position is defended by a much smaller group of sociologists, philosophers, and idealists. The weakness of these champions of social change lies in the fact that they make no practical proposals of ways and means for the conversion of the school into a great creative force in society. They confine their efforts very largely to the assertion that it should be so; the question of practical realization they leave to others; and others are not interested. As a consequence the probability is that the new curriculum, when completed, will enforce the principle of social conformity.

The Conception of Learning

The conception of learning which prevails most widely in the American school is the conception which has generally prevailed in the schools of the world. According to the tradition which has dominated formal education in the United States throughout its history learning is fundamentally a process of absorption. Through the centuries, according to this view, the race has accumulated a vast store of knowledge, the precipitate of experience, which must be passed on from generation to generation; and the major function of the school is to make certain that the child acquire in passive fashion this immensely valuable social heritage. He must *learn* the native language, the number system, the findings of the scientists, and the wise sayings of the prophets and sages, not through living but from the records of mankind. Thus learning becomes primarily an acceptance by the child of an externally imposed order and consequently an instrument of social conformity.

Against this conception of learning many of America's most able educational theorists have waged a vigorous warfare. These critics have argued that learning should not be regarded as the passive acquisition by the child of a body of skills, knowledges, and attitudes fixed by adult society, but that learning should be one aspect of an active process of living during which the child pursues ends immediately significant to him and thus gains a sense of mastery over rather than of submission to the social heritage. This means that the learner is brought squarely into the center of the picture.

At this point, however, the reformers break into two opposing camps. While both groups agree that economical and genuine learning is impossible without the interest and the active participation of the child, they differ radically on the question of the rôle which interest should play in the educative process. The more conservative group maintains that the good teacher so arranges the learning situation that the child will become interested in those things in which from the standpoint of society he should be interested; whereas the more radical group argues that the good teacher respects the spontaneous interests of the child and allows those interests to determine the direction which the process takes. At present the theory that learning is after all a matter of imposition, whether it is skillfully and efficiently or crudely and wastefully done, seems to be generally accepted in practice. Those who advocate the unqualified recognition of the interests of the learner have failed to show that they are not really defending a species of social anarchy. Moreover, except in a few private schools scattered here and there through the country, the more extreme theory has received little practical support.

Reliance upon the Textbook

One of the most characteristic features of American school procedure is reliance upon the textbook. This practice of course is in complete harmony with the traditional theory of learning. The textbook contains in condensed form the experience of the race in a particular department of knowledge. In times past the major task of the pupil was to memorize the contents of the textbook and that of the teacher was to determine the measure of success which had attended the pupil's efforts. To-day of course quite different methods for using the textbook generally prevail. There is much less emphasis on memoriter work than formerly and more time is devoted to discussion, sup-

plementary reading, individual projects, group enterprises, and laboratory work. Yet the textbook
remains an essential part of the American educational technique and the work of the school is still
closely identified with book learning.

That the wide use of the textbook tends to promote social conformity may not be altogether apparent at first. A brief examination of the practice, however, will show this to be true. In the first
place, the textbooks employed in a particular
school or school system are ordinarily selected lo-
cally. While this task is customarily performed by
teachers or committees of teachers, their selections
are of course subject to review by representatives
of the citizens serving on the board of education.
As a result no textbook is likely to be chosen which
offends the sensibilities of any group in the community that is sufficiently well organized to register a protest. In the second place, the publication
of textbooks is very largely in the hands of private
publishing companies which are conducted as business enterprises. Since these companies are interested in getting their own books adopted as widely
as possible, they very commonly bring pressure to
bear upon the authors to eliminate everything that
might be objectionable to any important body of
citizens in the nation. Moreover, the authors them-

selves have no doubt in many instances been easily convinced of the wisdom of leaving contentious matters out of their works. Thus a textbook in American history must not offend the Daughters of the American Revolution, the Knights of Columbus, the English Speaking Union, the United States Chamber of Commerce, the American Federation of Labor, the Grand Army of the Republic, the Order of Confederate Veterans, the American Legion, the Ku Klux Klan, and a host of other organizations. There have been numerous instances of the modification of textbooks at the request of some powerful group. Moreover, the same textbook has been issued in different editions to meet the demands of different sections of the country. Under these conditions the textbook tends to become a perfectly innocuous and colorless compendium of non-controversial knowledge and consequently an instrument of social conformity.

The Social Position of the Teacher

As a general rule the American teacher has not been an active force in the community. This is due largely to the fact that the financial compensation of the calling has been low and the consequent fact that the teacher has commonly been untrained and

immature. To-day, moreover, practically all of
the teachers in the elementary school and two-
thirds of the teachers in the secondary school are
women. Since woman has generally occupied a
position of inferiority in the economic, political,
and intellectual life of America, the profession
has as a consequence lacked prestige. Furthermore,
the absence of a comprehensive and thorough organization of teachers has made the individual
more or less helpless in the face of popular criticism. As a result of all of these conditions the
teacher, in the elementary and secondary schools
at any rate, has ordinarily been content to confine
his activities to the work of the classroom. In the
colleges and universities, to be sure, the situation is
somewhat different, but even here the influence of
social pressure may on occasion be keenly felt.

The American teacher is thus forced to resemble
the textbook. He is expected to lead a perfectly
exemplary life in order that he may set the proper
pattern for his pupils. But such a life, at least in
the smaller communities and the lower schools,
can only be the largest common factor of the various groups which make up the population. Since
the controlling forces in society and the publicly
expressed convictions of citizens tend to be conservative, this means that the teacher must be es-

sentially conservative in his behavior and opinions. Thus, in many of the smaller communities in the Middle West and South a teacher must not smoke, dance, or play cards, and, if he fails to attend church, he may be regarded with suspicion. Even such matters as the length of the dress, the bobbing of the hair, and the use of rouge have been known to disqualify a woman for teaching. And a shrewd observer of university life in America has said that there are three subjects on which the university professor is expected to be orthodox, that is, in accord with the powers which control higher education—economics, religion, and sex. According to this observer the professor may without greatly endangering his position overstep the bounds of propriety in one of these fields, but if he does so in a second, he is almost certain to be asked to seek employment elsewhere. While there may be some exaggeration in this statement, it contains sufficient truth to indicate that here is another factor which tends to make the school in America serve the interests of social conformity.

The Conservatism of the American People

In conclusion the point should be made that the school in America to-day is conservative because the American people are essentially conservative. The explanation of this situation is apparently to be found in the fact that the creative impulses which launched the republic on its course a century and a half ago have largely spent themselves. This does not mean that America has become the scene of rest and repose and quiet. The contrary is in fact the case. The concentration of power and energy in the United States to-day exceeds anything that the world has ever seen in the past. But this power and this energy are flowing in political channels and for social purposes which were fashioned in earlier generations. Moreover, interest in modifying the social structure is at a low ebb for the very reason that the present social structure has been successful according to the standards by which the American people pass judgment upon it. It has achieved material prosperity.

Although critics quite properly point to the great inequalities of wealth in the United States and to the existence of dire poverty in certain elements of the population, the fact remains that the American economic system has succeeded to an unprecedented degree in diffusing the goods and services of this world among the people. In the existing order those who have sufficient initiative and ability to organize and make their desires articulate are able to secure a share in the general prosperity. Those who lack this initiative and ability may experience severe physical privation, but, being unable to register effective protest, they are incapable of endangering the stability of the social structure. Moreover, many who are not prosperous to-day expect prosperity to-morrow and are therefore content. As a consequence, there is little organized unrest in contemporary America. The great masses of the people are therefore in no mood for radical political or economic doctrine. They firmly believe that, while crooks and scoundrels may find their way into high places from time to time, the American social system is fundamentally sound. Under these conditions, in spite of the demands of educational theorists that the school should serve as an agency of continuous social reconstruction, the forces of formal education tend to throw their weight on the side of social conformity.

CHAPTER IX

MECHANICAL EFFICIENCY

THE American people take great pride in their efficiency. Although this trait is to a very large degree a product of the new industrial civilization, it had its origin in the period of the pioneer. Under the hard conditions of life which accompanied the material conquest of Indians, forests, rivers, and mountains the formalities and leisurely ways of the Old World were perforce abandoned. The frontier nurtured simple and direct methods of work and of social procedure. Moreover, the abundance of natural resources of every kind and the sparseness of population placed a premium upon human labor, stimulated mechanical invention, and encouraged the utilization of non-human forms of power. Thus the large size of the farm in America and the scarcity of workers created an attitude of mind among the people which favored the rapid spread and universal adoption of farm machinery.

Building upon this foundation the new industrial order has provided in amazing abundance the tools of a certain type of efficiency. We say a certain type of efficiency, because it is often an efficiency without purpose, an efficiency of motion. To the Americans mechanical perfection is in itself something to admire and to strive for. If an organization or a machine works without undue friction or dissipation of energy, they would seem almost to be satisfied. America to-day consequently possesses a technique for the exploitation of natural resources, for the conservation of human power, for the fabrication of commodities, for the construction of bridges and skyscrapers, for the exchange of goods and services, for the raising of hogs and grain, for the transmission of thought and sound, and for the movement of huge populations to and fro, which surpasses anything of the kind that the world has seen. America is the land of locomotives, automobiles, telephones, labor-saving devices and gigantic industrial enterprise; she is also the land of wrist watches, time tables, electric bells, steam whistles, and cafeterias. The natural expectation is that this vast technique would guarantee leisure and tranquillity to all, but it seems rather to bring hurry and bustle and anxiety. To what humane ends therefore it will eventually be directed remains a mystery. For the moment the American people seem to be content with the mechanics of the accomplishment.

That this idolatry of efficiency should impress itself upon the schools is entirely to be expected. In fact, in those parts of the country which have come under the particular sway of the machine culture, the entire educational system and the accompanying educational theory have been greatly influenced by the ideals of business enterprise. Particularly in the great city systems education is thought of in terms of the construction of buildings, the floating of bonds, the keeping of records, the differentiation of function, and the evolution of a form of pupil management which makes possible the rapid and easy movement of great masses of children through the schools. And the ambitious school administrator covets a reputation for efficiency and feels complimented if he is mistaken for a banker or the director of some large corporation. Provided the ends are worthy there can of course be no objection to efficiency; but an efficiency of management should never be the ideal of education.

The Program of Mass Education

Perhaps the most characteristic expression of the concern of the Americans over efficiency is found in their program of mass education. This program of course is a product of the new industrial era. In the days of the agrarian civilization there was little mass education for the simple reason that schools and classes were necessarily small, the school year was short, attendance was irregular, and the program of studies was meager. Indeed before the coming of the great population centers and a closely integrated society, America never seriously undertook the task of providing schooling for the masses. Educational leaders, moreover, commonly contend that practically all of the progressive educational measures which have found their way into the schools during the past century appeared first in the cities. Only in the urban community with its concentration of children and its superior material resources could the problems of education be faced on a large scale.

Various obvious improvements in school practice, however, have been inevitably attended by methods of regimentation designed to deal with children in the mass. Thus the ordinary city system of education consists of a series of schools distributed over the city in accordance with the density of population and provided with comparatively little space for play and out-of-door activities. The buildings themselves are commonly huge structures equipped to take care of a thousand or more children. In the large cities schools housing several thousands of pupils are not uncommon, and at the secondary level the enrollment in a single school may reach the enormous figure of five, six, or even seven thousand. Under these conditions there is grave danger that the individual child will be lost and that the machinery of administration will obscure the process of education itself. That such results have appeared to a considerable degree in the American schools is clearly indicated by the numerous protests raised by educational theorists. But the momentum of the system, the demands of economy, and the resistance of vested interests within the school usually succeed in smothering criticism.

The controversy over size of class well illustrates the difficulties in the situation. In the elementary school forty and fifty children will be crowded into a single room and taught by a single teacher, and in the universities several hundred students will attend the same course of lectures. Although the cry has been raised again and again that genuine education is impossible under these conditions, the growth of the school population, the lag of the building program behind the need, and the cost of employing additional teachers make reform extremely difficult. Recently tradition has received unexpected support from scientific investigation. Studies have been made which purport to show that the results of instruction tend to sustain no relationship to the size of class and that children learn quite as well in large as in small groups. The researches have of necessity been limited to those educational products for the measurement of which objective tests and scales have been constructed. There is nevertheless a tendency in certain circles to assume either that the things measured are after all the central concern of the school or that they are intimately correlated with the less tangible, though perhaps even more desirable, educational products. But the theoretical battle over this issue is by no means concluded.

Flexible Classification and Promotion Arrangements

One of the first criticisms launched against the program of mass education was that it failed to make adequate provision for individual differences. In order to meet this criticism numerous schemes have been proposed and introduced into the schools. The American people, however, have been much more hospitable towards those mechanical devices of classification and promotion which make possible the easy manipulation of large numbers of pupils rather than towards those more fundamental reforms which center attention on the learning process. The suggestion therefore that instruction be adjusted to individual differences by making the individual the center of attention has usually fallen on deaf ears. On the other hand, schemes providing for a refinement of the methods of classification and the handling of children in groups have been readily accepted. Such schemes seem to be in harmony with the spirit which animates education in America. In the large cities now the pupils in a particular grade are often classified into a number of groups, commonly three, on the basis of ability, and then the materials of instruction and the rate of progress are adjusted to the several levels. This practice has the merit of recognizing to some extent differences in ability and of preserving the economies of mass production. It is also a reform that can be introduced rather easily from a central office without resorting to the laborious process of reëducating the teaching staff.

Perhaps, however, the methods which have been developed in the high schools and colleges for dealing with the great multitudes of young people who have poured into these institutions during the last generation are the most extreme illustrations of the application of the principle of mechanical efficiency to the processes of education. In both the secondary and higher schools the entire curriculum is organized into relatively minute units of work. Although efforts are always made to insure the pursuit on the part of the student of certain sequences and of a unified program, the result is all too often a mere collection of points or credits. Moreover, as the student remains in the institution from semester to semester his successes and failures in accumulating these precious credits are meticulously recorded even to fractions of percentages in some office or bureau. After he has acquired the appropriate number of such disparate units, with but little provision for the integration of his knowledge, he receives either his certificate of graduation from high school or his college degree. Even the granting of their highest academic honor, the degree of doctor of philosophy, has been reduced in certain of the large universities almost to a matter of meeting routine requirements. While this entire system has been the subject of severe criticism for some years and while numerous experiments in other directions are under way, it tends to remain because it is so well adapted to the demands of quantity production.

The Platoon Plan

Another interesting application of the principle of efficiency is found in the so-called platoon plan, which is designed for the elementary school, which has been very widely discussed in America, and which seems to be gaining ground in the great cities. In its essence the plan calls for an organization of the program that will make possible the continuous use throughout the day of the entire school plant. Under the traditional arrangement all children move simultaneously from the classroom to the playground, to the shops, or to the auditorium. As a consequence important parts of the school plant are always idle. Under the platoon plan, on the other hand, the pupils are divided into two shifts, and while the one is in the classrooms the other is in the shops, in the auditorium, and on the playground. The reform also provides for a modification of the program of instruction by placing larger emphasis upon play, manual, group, and various other activities. As a consequence certain of its protagonists have called it the *work-*

study-play plan. But undoubtedly the feature of the scheme which has appealed to those practical men who control public education in America is its provision for an efficient use of school resources.

In this connection the point should be made that the platoon plan is but one of several reforms which have made this particular appeal. For years numerous campaigns have been waged for the wider use of the school plant. At one time there has been a demand for converting the school into a community center for the benefit of the general population after the school day is over, at another for placing the school on Saturdays and even on Sundays at the disposal of any interested group of citizens, and again for maintaining a regular session of the school during the long summer vacation. All of these movements have met with some response, but boards of education have generally objected to incurring the extra expense which radical departures from tradition might entail. They have also hesitated to open the schools to religious gatherings or to partisan political meetings on the grounds that such practices are contrary to the purposes for which public schools are established.

The Measurement of School Products

During the past twenty-five or thirty years interest in the accurate measurement of school products has probably absorbed more energy and first-rate ability among students of education in America than any other single activity. Inspired by the technique which had been perfected in the natural sciences those engaged in this work have sought to standardize procedures and to improve instruments of testing so that the personal equation of the tester may be eliminated entirely. Beginning with the fundamental processes of arithmetic, reading, and spelling they have moved from discipline to discipline until they have produced objective tests for practically all subjects taught in the elementary and secondary schools. Even the curriculum of the college has not escaped altogether. And to-day efforts are being made to measure certain of the more subtle products of the educative process, such as attitudes and character traits. The guiding principle of this attempt to apply the quantitative method to education has thus been formulated by the recognized leader of the movement: *Whatever exists at all exists in some amount.* And the natural inference is that *whatever exists in some amount can be measured.*

Although the development of instruments for the measurement of school products has had a scientific as well as a practical motive, its major claim for popular support has been made in the name of efficiency. When the movement was in its first flush of youth its champions advanced the most extreme claims regarding its practical utility. Many school administrators and students of education apparently believed that measurement held the key to the solution of all educational problems. Through the use of standardized tests they argued that systems, schools, teachers, and methods could be appraised. An era of rapid and uninterrupted educational advance consequently seemed immediately ahead. The result was an orgy of testing that swept through the entire country.

While it is yet too early to appraise this movement in its entirety, certain conclusions may be drawn with confidence. As aids in the process of education and in the advancement of knowledge in the whole field of learning, instruments of measurement have proved their value and are certain to remain. On the other hand the feverish and uncritical fashioning of tests in terms of the existing curriculum and in the name of efficiency has undoubtedly served to fasten upon the schools an archaic program of instruction and a false theory of the nature of learning. There is also evidence to indicate that interest in standardized testing procedures has tended to stimulate the competitive impulses, to enforce social conformity, to mechanize the teaching process, and to center attention on the less important products of the school.

Scientific Management

The interest in the measurement of school products may be regarded as part of a more general concern over scientific management. And here students of education have borrowed directly from the field of industry. Impressed by the extraordinary increase in productive efficiency made possible by the analytical and objective study of factory processes and working methods, they concluded that the operations of a school or a school system might be approached in the same way and with the same beneficial results. As a consequence, with a view to eliminating waste of motion and duplication of effort, the functions of the different workers participating in the conduct of a great system of education have been carefully studied. Thus, the activities of janitors, classroom teachers, heads of departments, deans of girls, athletic directors, elementary school principals, secondary school principals, superintendents of schools, and members of school boards have all been made the subject of inquiry. While these investigations have brought many interesting facts to light, they have been too largely concerned with the machinery and the externals of education. They seem to have been betrayed by the analogy between school and industry from which they received their inspiration. In education there can never be that separation of process and product which is characteristic of manufacturing enterprise.

The method of scientific management has also been applied to the erection of school buildings, the making of equipment, the keeping of records, and the administration of finance. An elaborate technique for the selection of building sites in the light of probable population increases and movements has been evolved; standards with regard to lighting, ventilation, seating arrangements, corridor space, stairway provisions, and toilet facilities have been developed; and numerous studies of building materials, school supplies, and classroom equipment have been conducted. The process of record keeping has likewise been examined with great care, and efforts to perfect and standardize forms, blanks, and office devices have been made in great abundance. Also in quite recent years the entire field of school finance has been subjected to thorough scrutiny. And here the Americans have derived formulas which purport to reveal in an entirely objective fashion exactly how much money a community can afford to devote to educational purposes. Methods of apportioning funds, of financing various school projects, and other related problems have all been measured by the rod of efficiency. Even the costs per student hour of instruction in different subjects have been compared, and methods of equating various forms of educational service performed by teachers have been proposed. Certainly in their attack upon the material and routine aspects of school administration the Americans have shown great industry and ingenuity. Unfortunately, however, the same estimate cannot be passed upon their researches into the more fundamental relationships between school and society. The ideal of a narrow type of efficiency seems to have blinded them to wide areas of inquiry.

The Hierarchical Administrative Organization

The American interest in efficiency is well illustrated in the theory of administrative organization as it has developed in the cities. With few exceptions, the great population centers have repudiated directly and completely the principle of decentralization which has generally characterized the administration of education in the past. This is due largely to the fact that the system of public education in a community destined to become a great metropolis, keeping pace with the growth of population, becomes by imperceptible stages an undertaking of gigantic proportions. Moreover, with its thousands of teachers, its hundreds of thousands of pupils, and its millions of dollars worth of property, it takes on a superficial resemblance to big business. And since the efficiency of big business is generally praised in America, and since the board of education is commonly dominated by business men, the school system naturally adopts the administrative organization of business enterprise.

The organization which generally prevails in American cities is fundamentally hierarchical in form. In general charge of the school system, and responsible to the people precisely as the board of directors of a great corporation is responsible to the stockholders, is the board of education. And in the educational system, as in the corporate enterprise, below the controlling board is a systematically descending series of officers and workers.

Crowning this series is the official representative and executive of the board—the superintendent of schools. There then follow in order the assistant superintendents, the school principals, the heads of departments, the classroom teachers, and the pupils. Under this organization each individual in the system is responsible *to* the officer immediately over him and *for* all persons under him. The arrangement is thus perfectly logical in character and makes possible the definite placing of responsibility. Although certain liberal-minded theorists have criticized the theory underlying this system of administration on the grounds that it is undemocratic and tends to dwarf the personality of the teacher, the great majority of American students of the question maintain that it is the only system that will guarantee efficiency.

In this connection the exalted position of the administrator in the American scheme of education should be noted. Under the form of organization just outlined, which is generally found in the larger school systems and in the great universities, the superintendent of schools or the university president is far removed from the ordinary teacher. Moreover, being the immediate representative of the governing body in which teachers ordinarily have no voice, he wields enormous power. As a consequence, the more able young men in the service of public education are ambitious to become principals and superintendents, and a college professor who passes to a deanship or a presidency feels that he has been promoted. The status of teaching, on the contrary, tends to lose its traditional dignity and prestige; and the ordinary teacher comes to regard himself more and more in the nature of an employee and to view his work as lacking in creative opportunity. If these tendencies should continue, the Americans may expect that the profession increasingly will attract persons of little spirit and initiative.

Interest in the Tangible Symbols of Education

The natural fruit of this general absorption in the principle of efficiency divorced from a thoroughgoing inquiry into the purposes of human institutions is the glorification of the tangible symbols of education. Thus when the American people speak of the conditions of education in their country they commonly refer to figures of attendance, the number of degrees granted, the dollars spent on education, the size of school buildings, and even the exploits of the athletic teams rather than to the quality of the educative process and the excellence of the instruction. Their readiness to lavish money on school equipment and architecture and their reluctance to increase the compensation of teachers are to be understood in the same way. In a word they center the attention on the machinery and forms rather than on the substance of education. While this may be an inevitable product of the rapid expansion of the system of schools which has gone forward during the last generation, it is greatly hampering the fundamental reformulation of educational theory which the coming of industrialism has made imperative.

CHAPTER X

PRACTICAL UTILITY

THE forces in American life which produced the love of efficiency were also largely responsible for the development of a strong practical sense. Or perhaps we should say that the love of efficiency is one expression of the strong practical sense of the American people. A life close to nature for generations, combined with the fact that for the most part they had come originally from the uneducated classes of Europe, bred in them a genuine scorn of mere "book learning." Moreover, except for an ardent devotion to theology which persisted until the decline of the agrarian order and a keen interest in politics which was aroused by the founding of the nation and which spent itself in the nineteenth century, their preoccupation has always been with practical things. In the earlier epoch they were forced to fight savages, fell forests, break virgin soil, and erect dwellings; more recently they have been engrossed in the building of railroads, the digging of mines, the construction of factories, the manufacture of goods, and the sale of merchandise. The conquest of a continent within a century has placed a premium upon practical endeavor. And this concern with practical affairs has left its mark on the system of education.

Control of Education by Practical Men

Perhaps the most striking application of this principle of practical utility is the placing of the control of education in the hands of practical men. With the exception of the colonial period, when the voice of the clergy ruled the educational councils, it has always been so. To be sure, as we have already observed in another connection, power has not at all times resided in the same type of citizen. During the period of the district system educational policy, at least as it affected the lower schools, was determined almost altogether by small boards composed of farmers and rural artisans. But with the rise of industrialism and the development of cities the control of the public school in all of its forms, except in those regions where the district system still persists, has gradually come under the influence of the powerful commercial, financial, and industrial classes. The successful business man is the arbiter of educational enterprise in the United States to-day.

From the standpoint of the influence of the principle of practical utility, however, a clear line should be drawn between the earlier control by farmers and artisans and the later control by business men. The former seem to have been quite content to support the narrow academic type of education that had been bequeathed to them. Although they had little respect for book learning in the ordinary relationships of life, they regarded it as beyond their range of understanding—esoteric, mysterious, and imbued with magical power. The theory that the school should be made to serve the community and that the program of instruction should be related to ordinary life activities was consequently entirely foreign to their mode of thought. To them education was something apart, necessary for the training of clergymen and lawyers and professors, but of little practical concern to the man who worked with his hands in shop or field.

It is the business man, therefore, who has been chiefly responsible for the practical turn given to the educational program. Since the days of Benjamin Franklin, he has had visions of a system of education repudiating the narrow academic tradition of the clergy and the landed aristocracy and articulating boldly with the needs of industry and commerce and everyday life. He has therefore resolutely refused to follow the precedent established by the farmer and the artisan and sit in profound submission before this tradition of the court and the monastery. On the contrary the American business man has known his own mind and has sought to bend the school to his will. And since he has held the reins of power, while he may not always have pursued his ends wisely, he has succeeded in impressing his sense of practicality upon the entire system of public education. This does not mean, however, that he rejects altogether the theory that a special type of education without practical objective should be provided for those who can afford it. His first impulse may be to pursue such a course, but as his material position becomes more secure and he moves further and further from the masses who produced him he begins to see the merits of a special non-utilitarian education for the members of his class. Thus the most powerful and long-established families in America devote enormous sums of money every year to the luxurious maintenance of great private schools and colleges which give almost perfect expression to the aristocratic tradition in education. To these institutions the prosperous and class-conscious business man desires to send his own children.

The Low Regard for Intellectual Achievement

One of the most natural results of the rule of the practical man is the relatively low esteem in which disinterested intellectual achievement is held in America. To be sure, if this achievement gives promise of immediate utility, it is both highly prized and highly remunerated; but there is little store placed on that vast erudition in recondite fields which is the traditional possession of the scholar. As a consequence, while the applied sciences have flourished and have been supported with great generosity in the United States, the pure sciences and more abstract disciplines have languished. Even the arts have been forced to choose between extinction and the service of practical ends. The great rewards everywhere have gone to those who have been willing to devote their talents to the development of industry and the achievement of material prosperity. And so strong has been this utilitarian urge that the world of business tends to attract an undue proportion of gifted men.

Abundant evidence of the low regard for intellectual attainments may be found in American colleges and universities. While there are of course many exceptions to the rule, these institutions are not devoted primarily to scholarship and the advancement of learning. At least this may be said of the great undergraduate colleges leading to the baccalaureate. Here the interests which really evoke the energies of the students are social rather than intellectual. It is about the athletic contests, the fraternities, the dramatic societies, the school papers, and the various clubs rather than about the arts and the sciences that the life of the institution actually revolves. Leadership in these student activities is therefore commonly prized above eminence in scholarship. Moreover, the motive which brings the young man or woman to college is less a love of learning than a desire to participate in the student life, to form desirable social connections, and to discover the road to personal success.

These shortcomings of the higher education, if such they be, are already recognized by American educational leaders and are the subject of endless comment and criticism. Moreover, numerous experiments, designed to stimulate interest in intellectual things and ranging all the way from the introduction of the English tutorial system to the organization of special courses on how to study, have been launched; but the forces with which such experiments are seeking to grapple have their root far beyond college halls in the very fabric of society. When a man of great wealth is able to found a college or university and employ an entire staff of professors, or when a board of trustees composed of men of little learning pass unfavorable judgment, as they sometimes do, on the work of a famous scholar, a student of very modest wit will have little difficulty in distinguishing the real source of power or in sensing the actual standards of worth which prevail in America. And youth, unless he possesses an unusually strong intellectual bent, will scarcely be attracted by the career of the university professor.

Many Americans argue, however, that the coming of the practical man into the sphere of education has been of untold benefit. Admitting that it has been attended by genuine evils, they contend that it has overthrown many an ancient academic fetish, that it has exposed the sterility and empty pretensions of various scholastic traditions, and that it has brought education into the service of society and the ordinary needs of men. In a word, they maintain that it has tended to deflate the academic mind and to drive much of the pious humbug out of university halls. In this estimate there is no doubt much of truth. The spokesmen of the new dispensation, moreover, say that, as

American civilization matures, the need for an intellectual class and for the prosecution of the more fundamental types of inquiry will make itself felt. They also have a ready answer to the query regarding the wisdom of entrusting the control of education so completely to one element in the population. The business men of America, having succeeded according to the prevailing social standards, are in a sense the most faithful representatives of society and the most reliable trustees of its welfare. They are therefore the natural guardians of its future and the logical architects of its educational system.

The Sensitivity of the School to Social Demand

Although American educators are constantly complaining that educational practice tends to lag far behind social change and is slow to respond to the needs of society, as a matter of fact the school in the United States has shown an extraordinary readiness to obey any clearly expressed demand on the part of society. In the past, to be sure, it has rarely taken the initiative and sought to anticipate the social will. On the contrary, it has ordinarily awaited a clear mandate from society or some responsible social group. The response of the school may not be in accord with the most approved theory of education or in harmony with the formulations of idealists; but no one can observe the American educational system for a year without being impressed by its truly extraordinary sensitivity to the social *milieu*. The American secondary school, for example, long ago abandoned the classical tradition which still holds the secondary schools of Western Europe in its grip. The subject of Greek has almost completely disappeared, and Latin, though continuing to occupy a fairly important position in the curriculum, is distinctly on the defensive. Moreover, the entire program of instruction in the public high school to-day is in a state of flux: new subjects are being added and old subjects are being dropped with great rapidity. Any proposal that has the semblance of rationality, provided it does not run counter to some powerful social force, is almost certain somewhere to be given a trial in the program.

The growth of the extra-curriculum activities in secondary school and college during the last generation and a half also shows the extent to which the educational system will respond to popular demands. In its beginnings this movement encountered nothing but hostility or indifference from the members of the instructional staff.

Nevertheless, because it received popular support and constituted an adjustment to a new epoch in American society, it quickly prevailed over all academic opposition. And now these activities are not only tolerated by the teaching profession, but, except in their more extreme manifestations, are even defended as a sound and desirable educational reform. They have become a recognized part of the school or college program, and persons to organize and direct them are being trained in the universities and teachers colleges every year. Thus, largely because of social pressure, what was opposed a generation ago is to-day given a place of honor in the educational system.

The institutions of higher learning in America also reveal in unmistakable fashion the readiness with which the most sacred academic traditions will give way before the popular will. The great state university, for example, which can trace its lineage back to the most conservative universities of Europe, will teach any subject for which there is an organized demand. In its broad program of instruction the inquisitive observer may find anything from Radio to Sanskrit, although the chances are that he will find the former more frequently than the latter. This institution, moreover, has not been permitted to remain within its own walls: it has been forced to go out into the most remote corners of the state and to organize extension courses for both old and young. So varied are the activities of the American university and so careless are its standards of scholarship that the visitor from Europe is inclined to deny to it the right to be called a university. This is no doubt often humiliating to the American professor, but the people through their practical-minded representatives go blithely on their way requiring of the university whatsoever seems good to them. They may even pass a law compelling the university to admit any student who has been graduated from a public high school within the state. And the university has no recourse.

This sensitivity to social demand the Americans rightly regard as one of the great merits of their educational system. The intimacy of the relationship between the school and the people renders impossible that sanctification of academic tradition which has so frequently destroyed the vitality of educational institutions. One naturally wonders, however, whether the school in the United States may not be sensitive to the fluctuations and the eddies rather than to the deep-flowing currents of the social stream. Under present conditions educational changes may represent a response to surface phenomena or the passions of the moment. Thus, during the World War, as we have seen, the German language was thrown out of the secondary schools, and since the opening of the century the teaching of Spanish has spread with great rapidity apparently on the groundless assumption that it is essential to the development of commercial relations with Latin America. In other words, the present sensitivity of the school, with all of its merits, tends to make the educational system the happy hunting ground for every agency of propaganda in the United States.

The Doctrine of Specific Training

The principle of practical utility has received quite unexpected support from a long series of learning experiments conducted by American psychologists since the nineties of the last century. These investigations have been interpreted as proving that learning is specific rather than general, that the development of facility in one field of endeavor is of little value in another, and that, in a word, all talk about training the mind should be regarded on the same plane as belief in witchcraft. Thus were destroyed the foundations upon which the old classical education had rested in

America. According to the view which had formerly prevailed in academic circles and which had been generally accepted by the ordinary citizen, probably because the line of reasoning was difficult to follow and was supported by the prestige of great names, the study of Latin and Greek and Mathematics develops in the student general mental powers which are then available for service in various spheres of practical endeavor.

The educational implications of the new doctrine were quickly grasped by the American people and proved to be entirely congenial to their temper. When they were told by eminent psychologists that the study of Latin merely gives facility in Latin and the study of Trigonometry facility in Trigonometry, the argument appealed to their practical sense and the scene was laid for a new attack upon the curriculum. Being convinced that education should prepare for the real activities of life and being convinced further now that the only sound method of preparation is through direct participation in these activities, they were forced to turn for guidance to an examination of contemporary society. The logical result was the development of the technique of job or activity analysis. According to this method life as it is lived to-day in America should be analyzed into its separate activities and the school program should be compounded in some fashion from the findings. The underlying assumption is that learning is specific and that faith in the development of general intellectual powers is educational superstition.

At the present time, however, the Americans find themselves in a serious dilemma. They have come to realize that they are living in the most dynamic civilization of history and that the world about them is undergoing constant transformation. Obviously the doctrine of specific training, the doctrine of psychological mechanism, the doctrine that all learning is essentially the formation within the nervous system of bonds between particular situations and particular responses, the doctrine which was welcomed half a generation ago as the sure road to educational salvation, makes no provision for adjustment to a changing civilization. As a consequence, educators find themselves constrained to prepare the coming generation for the rapidly shifting scenes of industrialism with a psychology which implies that this is impossible. They are therefore turning to the reëxamination of theories once discarded and the formulation of a new theory of learning.

Interest in the Scientific Study of Education

Without doubt the finest educational fruit which the practical sense of the American people has borne is the movement for the scientific study of education. Discarding the older purely speculative approach to the problems of the school, which was never in harmony with their spirit, they began near the close of the last century to apply the scientific method to the study of the learning process. From this simple beginning the movement spread from field to field until to-day there is practically no division of the educational domain which has not been touched. The native equipment of the individual, methods of learning, teaching procedures, curriculum construction, school administration, the relations of school to society, and even the aims of education have all been made the subject of objective inquiry. The result has been the accumulation of a vast amount of more or less reliable knowledge about education and the development of numerous instruments of research and techniques of investigation.

The Americans, with few exceptions, have the utmost confidence in the application of the scientific method to the field of education. Many prominent educators seem even to believe that there is no educational problem which is incapable of objective solution. They contend, moreover, that insistence on the employment of any other method is to waste time and obscure thinking. In support of this position they point to the centuries of fruitless speculation about education and to the general disrepute into which such speculation plunged the entire subject of pedagogy. They consequently demand facts, and yet more facts; and the surest and quickest way of achieving academic reputation among them is either to collect or to devise some instrument for collecting new facts. They, however, never define very clearly just what they mean by facts, and how facts are to be distinguished from ideas. Because of this deep distrust of speculation there are great university departments of education in the United States in which no general courses in educational philosophy or the general theory of education are offered. The Americans thus hope to make education an exact science and remove its problems from the realm of dispute.

This complete absorption in educational science, however, is beginning to relax. Many able students of the question are contending that the solution of educational problems does not follow automatically from investigation and that provision must be made for a process of synthesis and evaluation which lies somewhat beyond the confines of science. They argue that, while facts are absolutely essential to the solution of an educational problem, the same facts may with different sets of values lead to different solutions. In other words, they maintain that the facts must be brought into harmony with some theory of what is good and just and beautiful, and must be definitely related to some particular order of society. This point of view, however, which would deny the thesis that there is any single solution to an educational problem, occupies a minority position in America to-day.

Educational Instrumentalism

The highest expression of the American principle of practical utility is found in the universal tendency to regard the function of education as being essentially instrumental. The people of the United States almost never view education as a way of life or of personal culture. They rather look upon it as an external means for the attainment of some definite and desirable goal. Thus when they formulate the aims of the school they habitually refer to the improvement of this or that aspect of life. They say that the school should promote sound health, elevate the family relationship, train for vocational efficiency, prepare for good citizenship, develop worthy recreational habits, purify the moral and religious life, or do something else for the advancement of the individual or society.

This interest of the Americans in utility of course harmonizes with their penchant for practical idealism and their general faith in progress. At the same time their instrumentalism is relatively ineffective, except on a very narrow scale, because they can agree on no fundamental conception of progress beyond the promotion of individual success. Even when they speak of good citizenship or worthy home membership they are able to secure popular support only so long as they put traditional content into the terms. Thus, in spite of their extreme practicality, in the realm of the organization of educational purposes they tend to seek refuge in the social platitudes coined in the days of the agrarian culture and to avoid that vast range of truly disturbing problems raised by the advent of industrial civilization.

CHAPTER XI

PHILOSOPHIC UNCERTAINTY

THE analysis of the theory that underlies and supports the American educational structure may well be closed by an examination of what may be called the principle of philosophic uncertainty. Although there are many elements in that structure which represent a strongly contrary theoretical position, this principal may be regarded as distinctly characteristic of the American way of thought on educational matters. Moreover, it would seem to penetrate not only their theory of education, but also their entire theory of society. It is found in their mistrust of government, in their championship of private initiative, in their opposition to centralization, in their faith in the scientific method, in their fondness for pragmatism in philosophy, in their rejection of authoritarianism, and in their general lack of confidence in rigid formulas.

The point is of course readily conceded that this principle represents American thought at its best and does not embrace all that goes on in the United States. It does not, for example, harmonize with the worship of the fathers of the constitution, the passage of the prohibition amendment, the crusades of the fundamentalists, the enactment of laws for the regulation of moral conduct, and the general behavior of the American people during the Great War. Nor is it in accord with many of the educational tendencies which have been described in this volume. It will nevertheless serve as a useful and appropriate caption under which certain of the most characteristic aspects of the American theory of education may be examined.

The Absence of Social Planning

American society is not planned: it grows in response to the drive of internal forces and within the limits set by external circumstance and the interaction of its various members. Only in times of severe national crisis is any general effort made to secure unified and concerted action in a particular direction. According to the American theory of government the function of the state is to regulate and not to organize and administer the affairs of the nation. Although the individual commonwealth and the federal union have both gradually increased the scope of their activities, yet it remains substantially true that American society

possesses neither the will nor the means for planning the general evolution of the social structure. The entire history of the country from the days of the pioneer down to the age of the automobile is a record of the achievements of the uncoördinated and spontaneous efforts of individuals and groups. Even the school system, though exhibiting a certain logic, was never planned as a whole. Whatever of uniformity there may be in educational practice from one part of the nation to another is therefore the product of a common cultural tradition, similar geographical surroundings, facts of communication, and unity of social purpose.

With this policy of permitting social institutions to evolve in obedience to their own laws the American people generally are in hearty agreement. They look upon any effort to design and direct the evolution of society as utterly Utopian. According to their view all attempts at planning are certain to fail because the modern social order is so complex and dynamic that no man or group of men has sufficient wisdom to bring the vast range of its processes under orderly control. If the attempt to perform such a superhuman task were ever made, either the most pertinent facts would be overlooked or the situation would change so rapidly that the data in hand would always falsify

the living situation. The Americans contend, moreover, that if men had sufficient wisdom to plan on such a gigantic scale, they would lack the necessary moral integrity. Those to whom the task would be delegated could not be trusted to employ their power in the interests of the whole of society. And in support of this thesis reference is made to the innumerable instances in history where small groups have grievously betrayed the general good and used power to promote their own selfish ends. The American people therefore prefer to place their faith in the irrational rather than in the rational forces of society. They prefer blind chance checked here and there by collective action, to any general effort at the reasoned ordering of social life.

The way in which this theory of society affects education is fairly obvious. If America has no social program, the schools can have no such program. As a consequence the promotion of an intimate and functional relationship between school and society becomes difficult and the teaching of patriotism tends to assume a negative form. Since society as a whole, whether it be community, state, or nation, seldom launches any collective enterprise, except the waging of a foreign war, the staging of an athletic contest, or the curbing of

some peculiarly flagrant form of crime or corruption, patriotic instruction must lack concrete and positive objective. To be told that the highest patriotism is to be a good citizen, when citizenship in times of peace provides little opportunity to engage in large creative undertakings, can make but little appeal to the spirit and imagination of youth. Since war is the only really great enterprise in which the country as a whole participates, the American people naturally tend to identify patriotism with willingness to bear arms in defense of the nation. Patriotism also commonly embraces reverence for the major political and military heroes of the past, loyalty to the constitution, and faith in the essential justice and goodness of American institutions. And the schools, since they can have no tangible social goal, must center their attention primarily on helping the individual to succeed. The constant efforts of numerous theorists to impress upon the system of education the ideal of service to society have consequently moderated but little the powerful drive towards personal success. The fact that the only possible method of reducing the strength of this force is to provide for it a practicable substitute has apparently not been sensed.

The Play of Social Forces

The refusal of American society as a whole to plan its future, however, does not imply a general absence of planning in the United States. Men can of course no more refrain from attempting to control the course of events by taking thought than they can abstain from eating and drinking and sleeping. As individuals and as groups the American people have always schemed and planned for the future. Moreover, as society has become more complex, the number, the self-consciousness, and the organic cohesion of these groups have correspondingly increased. To-day the nation literally seethes with organizations and societies each bent on the attainment of some end which it regards as legitimate or desirable. There are organizations of farmers, of carpenters, of longshoremen, of manufacturers, of bankers, of physicians, of lawyers, of clergymen, of teachers, of bootleggers, of prohibitionists, of women, of Methodists, of Catholics, of Jews, of Irishmen, of Germans, of Chinese, of Negroes, and hundreds of other groups bound together by community of interest and aspiration. And every one of these organizations has its plans which it seeks to further.

In some cases it speaks boldly and unashamedly in its own name, while in others it frames its petitions in terms of the public good. But the point worthy of attention is that, whatever its motive or method, it endeavors to mold the world according to its own desires.

These groups, moreover, have not failed to observe the system of public education. As they have grown and become more articulate, the school has developed into a social institution of the first rank. Recognizing the enormous power which it is capable of wielding they have sought to secure its services. Every school system in the United States therefore, and particularly in the large cities, is the center upon which social forces are constantly playing. Scarcely a day or a week passes that the board of education or the superintendent of schools or some organization of teachers is not approached by the representative or representatives of one of these groups of citizens who would like to alter school programs or policies. Sometimes they demand the dismissal of a teacher, sometimes they ask for the modification of the curriculum, and sometimes they seek material advantage in the purchase or sale of property.

According to the orthodox American theory all of these efforts of private citizens to shape the program of public education are illegitimate and not to be allowed. But just how such efforts are to be thwarted is a problem which seems to defy solution. Moreover, the struggle among the various external forces is by no means an equal contest, and there is little reason for believing that the cause of righteousness will prevail. Because of the enormous economic power which they customarily control and the great social prestige which they commonly enjoy, the more conservative forces, unless they overstep the bounds of propriety, tend to be victorious. As a consequence liberal-minded educators and laymen have banded themselves together from time to time to keep what they call pernicious and reactionary influences out of the school. The ebb and flow of this struggle, however, seems but to reflect the ebb and flow of the larger struggle which goes on in society.

The Separation of Education and Politics

In certain educational quarters this interest in protecting the school against the play of social forces has taken the extreme form of advocating the complete separation of education and politics. Indeed the theory of school administration which is now most strongly intrenched in the colleges of education in America champions this view. The thesis is even advanced that one of the distinctive characteristics of the evolution of public education in the United States is its freedom from the operation of political influences. And, since the school everywhere has developed as a community enterprise, it is undoubtedly true that the great national political parties have devoted but little attention to education. This entire discussion, however, seems to be somewhat confused because of the two senses in which the term *politics* is used. Thus, some writers, following the tradition of scholarship, employ it to embrace all of those activities of society which aim to give expression to the collective will, while others apply it only to those perversions of politics which involve the subordination of the public interest to the personal fortunes of politicians and office-seekers.

Concerning the desirability of protecting the school from the predatory assaults of political adventurers and scoundrels there can of course be no divergence of opinion. But to insist further that the school should be placed beyond the reach of those forces which are constantly remaking the structure of society is quite another matter. In fact, since education must always be one of the major concerns of any advanced culture, it should be recognized as one of the central problems of politics. That a contrary position should be taken by the educational leaders of a nation such as America which spends more than two billions of dollars annually on its schools indicates either a very inferior order of politics or a strange conception of the nature of education. The explanation is indeed to be traced to both of these factors.

Organized politics in America has reached a stage of almost complete ideological bankruptcy. There are, to be sure, two venerable political parties which engage in contests for office from year to year, but students of political science experience the greatest difficulty in distinguishing the one from the other except in terms of personalities and historical tradition. Neither has a social program of any substance; both appeal to the electorate on the grounds of prosperity; and each promises more of this particular commodity than the other. Consequently, until there is a realignment of political forces in the United States, the welfare of public education undoubtedly demands that the unenlightened struggles for office of these two parties be removed as far from the schools as possible. Under present conditions the policy followed in many American communities of holding separate school elections and of organizing non-partisan boards of education, that is, boards composed equally of representatives of both parties, possesses genuine merit. Nevertheless, this is at best a direct evasion of the problem and must fail utterly to provide that articulation with social purpose upon which the vitality of education depends. And the observation should be made here that school and politics have not always been separated in the United States. In fact the long and bitterly contested struggle which resulted in the establishment of the great state systems of public education in the second quarter of the nineteenth century was essentially a political struggle.

America, however, is not as bankrupt politically as an examination of the behavior of the two great parties would indicate. Certainly, whatever may have been the situation in the past, these parties to-day are not the centers of power. A moment's reflection on the extraordinary complexity of life in the United States is sufficient to reveal the artificiality of any division of the electorate into two opposing groups. The authentic political forces are therefore found outside the parties in those numerous organized groups to which reference has already been made. These groups are the active and vital political influences in the nation; and, as we have seen, they are not disposed to leave the schools alone. We may assume, moreover, that so long as they exist as living members of society they are certain to take a hand in the formulation of educational policy. The need in America to-day is not to deny the validity of such forces but rather to provide the channels through which they may find full and balanced expression.

The demand on the part of the Americans that the school be separated from politics is also supported by a strange notion regarding the nature of education which prevails among them. In some of their pronouncements they seem to regard education as possessing a pure and independent quality which removes it from the passions generated by social conflict and which gives it a sort of transcendent authority in human affairs. Whether this authority is derived from the laws of child nature, from certain methods inherent in education itself, or from the superior wisdom of the profession of teaching is never made entirely clear. They nevertheless tend to agree in the abstract that education is to be distinguished clearly and radically from all forms of propaganda and that the latter are the natural and inevitable consequence of the incursion of political forces into the school. This position may perhaps be clarified by examining the widespread notion that indoctrination is undesirable and dangerous.

The Fear of Indoctrination

In general the American people express a fear of using the schools for purposes of indoctrination. In the great majority of cases, however, this fear is found only in its naïve form. Like other peoples the world over they firmly believe that they are in a sense the chosen people of God, that their culture is obviously superior to all others, and that their institutions are the pure product of human reason. Moreover, these views are commonly held by every group, sect, or locality in the country. As a consequence, when any segment of the American people teach to their children that their views of the universe, from the functions of the county sheriff to the destiny of man, are good, true, and right, they do not feel that they are indoctrinating the coming generation with the peculiar set of beliefs which they have inherited from their fathers. To be sure, when they behold their neighbors behaving in similar fashion, they recognize the process at once as indoctrination of the most dangerous and unjustifiable character; but when they behave thus themselves they sincerely believe that they are merely guarding their boys and girls from error.

American educators, however, are developing a more thoughtful form of opposition to indoctrination in the schools. They begin by defining indoctrination as the authoritative teaching of any attitude or belief as fixed, final, and unchanging. But the theory underlying their opposition to such a method of instruction takes different forms at the hands of different writers. Some seem to rest their case largely on the sentimental argument that helpless little children should not be imposed upon by their elders. They appear to regard with genuine horror anything that resembles the molding of the child according to a preconceived pattern. Just why imposition of this character, regardless of the quality of the pattern selected, is undesirable is a question which remains unanswered. It would seem that any imposition which society might make upon the child through the school is a small matter in comparison with the imposition of which the parents are guilty in bringing the child into the world at a particular point in time and place and endowed with a particular set of inborn qualities. Perhaps these critics are inbred with a strong sense of justice and feel compelled to come to the support of the child in his supposed

unequal struggle with the adult world; perhaps
they have a faith in the essential goodness of child
nature and the essential evil of society; or perhaps
they have concluded from experience that better
human beings are developed under the conditions
of freedom which they advocate. They should
observe, however, that the order of society implicit
in their proposals is anarchy, and that in shaping
the environment in which they place the child they
are imposing their adult wills upon him just as
surely as though they taught him a particular
doctrine about the universe.

Other opponents of narrow forms of indoctrination who make the nature of modern society their
point of departure seem to be standing on much
firmer ground. They begin with the thesis that the
spread of science has given to modern civilization
a dynamic quality which no past culture has possessed in anything like the same degree. They
argue very cogently therefore that the indoctrination of the child with a set of fixed beliefs and
attitudes is to unfit him for life in the world as
it is. Since nothing is stable in the external environment, the individual should have a mental
equipment which is highly sensitive to change and
capable of rapid adjustment. He should be as
ready to adopt new ideas and points of view as to

install the most up-to-date labor saving devices in his dwelling or to introduce the latest inventions into his factory. Undoubtedly, although this theory may be carried to absurd extremes, that strange industrial civilization which is sweeping America and the world is placing a premium increasingly on the elastic mind.

This doctrine, however, contains a certain weakness or a peculiar reflection of the American situation which should not be overlooked. Life in the republic, as we have seen, is dominated to a very unusual degree by the ideal of individual success. Now, if the individual is to succeed according to current standards in a civilization which is changing as rapidly as that found in the United States, he must indeed possess a very flexible mind. He must be capable of keeping abreast of the swiftly moving procession of ideas, fashions, and inventions. But a society which is dominated less by the thought of individual advancement and more by certain far-reaching purposes and plans for social construction might find a firmer and more steadfast mentality desirable. Thus, at the very time that the Americans are becoming fearful of all forms of indoctrination they may be in danger of becoming completely victimized and molded by the mechanics of industrialism. There is indeed some reason for believing that civilization in the United States is losing that moral quality or passion which gives the central meaning to life.

The Doctrine of Academic Freedom

The theoretical opposition of the Americans to indoctrination and their insistence on the separation of education and politics find expression at the higher levels of the educational system in the doctrine of academic freedom. In its pure form this doctrine maintains not only that the school should be separated from the play of political forces but also that the university is in a very genuine sense above politics. Thus the institution of higher learning is dedicated to the free and unprejudiced search after truth, as well as to teaching and professional training. The theory underlying the doctrine is that, in the long run and regardless of existing institutional forms, the best interests of society will be served by the courageous and unhampered prosecution of inquiry in every sphere of knowledge and human activity. Truth, moreover, tends to be regarded as possessing an absolute rather than a relative quality. It is a familiar doctrine and one which universities have sought to uphold in many countries for generations.

The ideal as outlined is of course far from realized in America to-day. In the field of the more abstract disciplines and sciences, such as philology, mathematics, and physics, there is practically complete freedom of research, publication, and teaching. In other areas of knowledge, however, the situation may be quite different. In the realm of biology, for example, while there is comparatively little coercion, even in the great universities study of sex phenomena may be censored and in the smaller institutions of the culturally more retarded regions the teaching of evolution may be strictly forbidden. But it is in the department of the strictly human sciences, such as economics, political science, and sociology, that there exists the largest measure of restriction. The degree of such restriction varies of course from time to time. During periods of crisis the area of freedom may be greatly reduced, while in times of unusual security it may be equally widely extended. Occasionally professors are dismissed because of their radical teaching, but the more usual method of securing conformity is to withhold promotion and to trust that the advancing years and the subtle forces of social suggestion will cool the hot passions and moderate the fervent idealisms of youth. Those who defend this curtailment of liberty argue that progress must be made slowly and that ideas in the field of social relations are peculiarly dangerous. The real explanation, however, seems to be that the complete separation of education and politics, even in the somewhat rarefied atmosphere of the university, is very difficult to achieve.

There is one aspect of the American education program which merits special mention in this connection. The decentralization of the control and administration of higher education in the United States undoubtedly makes for freedom. A professor who is dismissed from the faculty of one university because of his radical tendencies may be invited to join the faculty of a neighboring institution. Certain universities are notoriously conservative, while others have a long liberal tradition. Moreover, within the same institution some departments will be reactionary and others radical. And a very modest degree of radicalism or originality along certain lines, commonly referred to as progressive spirit, is quite generally encouraged. Under these conditions, unless he attacks long and vigorously the foundations of the American social order, the university professor is unlikely to experience serious infringements on his liberty as a scholar. Yet the fact that the control of higher education seems to be passing increasingly into the hands of business men and the further fact that the same individuals, men of great financial power and influence, may serve on the boards of trustees of several different institutions tend to bring the universities more completely under the domination of a particular class —and a class which is peculiarly interested in maintaining the existing social order.

The Principle of Philosophic Uncertainty

Being dominated in its ideology by a strongly positivistic and agnostic tradition American educational theory to-day seems to be permeated with a general attitude of philosophic uncertainty. In some measure, as the foregoing analysis plainly shows, the uncertainty is an attitude of mind deliberately adopted; but in a larger measure it seems to reflect the condition of life as a whole in the United States. Industrialism, having swept away the material foundations of the ancestral order, is now fast destroying the entire system of morals and beliefs which that order nourished and supported. The American people are consequently between two civilizations and are the inevitable victims of doubt and uncertainty. The intellectual classes have abandoned the old and as yet have not created a new outlook upon the world. Education therefore, like other departments of life, faces an enormous task of construction.

The first reaction of educational leaders in the United States to this situation appears to be in essence an evasion of the problem. The most that they have done thus far is to formulate a philosophy of negation which at best can serve only to facilitate the demolition of the old order. However, it seems entirely possible that, moved by the best of intentions, they will unwittingly serve the purposes of that unnatural offspring of the union of the agrarian and industrial civilizations—the ardent worship of mechanical efficiency, practical utility, and individual success. Afraid of social forces, fearful of indoctrination, and trustful of experience, they refuse to give the positive guidance which is the only alternative to superficiality and drift. Indeed, the policy of refusing to attempt clear and unequivocal formulations of educational policy may result in surrendering the field to the forces of social and political reaction.

American education to-day, like American society at large, is in need of a conception of life suited to the new civilization. Most of the ideal terminology which students of education currently employ, if it is positive in quality, is the heritage from the earlier society. Since this terminology, however, is a product of a social order that has passed away, it ordinarily lacks both color and substance. Much is said in American educational circles to-day about democracy, citizenship, and ethical character, but nowhere can be found bold and creative efforts to put real content into these terms. In a word, the educational and social implications of the machine culture have not been thought through. And until the leaders of educational thought in America go beyond the gathering of educational statistics and the prosecution of scientific inquiry, however valuable and necessary these undertakings may be, and grapple courageously with this task of analysis and synthesis, the system of education will lack direction and the theory of education will but reflect the drift of the social order.

AMERICAN EDUCATION:
ITS MEN, IDEAS, AND INSTITUTIONS

An Arno Press/New York Times Collection

Series I

Adams, Francis. The Free School System of the United States. 1875.

Alcott, William A. Confessions of a School Master. 1839.

American Unitarian Association. From Servitude to Service. 1905.

Bagley, William C. Determinism in Education. 1925.

Barnard, Henry, editor. Memoirs of Teachers, Educators, and Promoters and Benefactors of Education, Literature, and Science. 1861.

Bell, Sadie. The Church, the State, and Education in Virginia. 1930.

Belting, Paul Everett. The Development of the Free Public High School in Illinois to 1860. 1919.

Berkson, Isaac B. Theories of Americanization: A Critical Study. 1920.

Blauch, Lloyd E. Federal Cooperation in Agricultural Extension Work, Vocational Education, and Vocational Rehabilitation. 1935.

Bloomfield, Meyer. Vocational Guidance of Youth. 1911.

Brewer, Clifton Hartwell. A History of Religious Education in the Episcopal Church to 1835. 1924.

Brown, Elmer Ellsworth. The Making of Our Middle Schools. 1902.

Brumbaugh, M. G. Life and Works of Christopher Dock. 1908.

Burns, Reverend J. A. The Catholic School System in the United States. 1908.

Burns, Reverend J. A. The Growth and Development of the Catholic School System in the United States. 1912.

Burton, Warren. The District School as It Was. 1850.

Butler, Nicholas Murray, editor. Education in the United States. 1900.

Butler, Vera M. Education as Revealed By New England Newspapers prior to 1850. 1935.

Campbell, Thomas Monroe. The Movable School Goes to the Negro Farmer. 1936.

Carter, James G. Essays upon Popular Education. 1826.

Carter, James G. Letters to the Hon. William Prescott, LL.D., on the Free Schools of New England. 1824.

Channing, William Ellery. Self-Culture. 1842.

Coe, George A. A Social Theory of Religious Education. 1917.

Committee on Secondary School Studies. Report of the Committee on Secondary School Studies, Appointed at the Meeting of the National Education Association. 1893.

Counts, George S. Dare the School Build a New Social Order? 1932.

Counts, George S. The Selective Character of American Secondary Education. 1922.

Counts, George S. The Social Composition of Boards of Education. 1927.

Culver, Raymond B. **Horace Mann and Religion in the Massachusetts Public Schools.** 1929.

Curoe, Philip R. V. **Educational Attitudes and Policies of Organized Labor in the United States.** 1926.

Dabney, Charles William. **Universal Education in the South.** 1936.

Dearborn, Ned Harland. **The Oswego Movement in American Education.** 1925.

De Lima, Agnes. **Our Enemy the Child.** 1926.

Dewey, John. **The Educational Situation.** 1902.

Dexter, Franklin B., editor. **Documentary History of Yale University.** 1916.

Eliot, Charles William. **Educational Reform: Essays and Addresses.** 1898.

Ensign, Forest Chester. **Compulsory School Attendance and Child Labor.** 1921.

Fitzpatrick, Edward Augustus. **The Educational Views and Influence of De Witt Clinton.** 1911.

Fleming, Sanford. **Children & Puritanism.** 1933.

Flexner, Abraham. **The American College: A Criticism.** 1908.

Foerster, Norman. **The Future of the Liberal College.** 1938.

Gilman, Daniel Coit. **University Problems in the United States.** 1898.

Hall, Samuel R. **Lectures on School-Keeping.** 1829.

Hall, Stanley G. **Adolescence: Its Psychology and Its Relations to Physiology, Anthropology, Sociology, Sex, Crime, Religion, and Education.** 1905. 2 vols.

Hansen, Allen Oscar. **Early Educational Leadership in the Ohio Valley.** 1923.

Harris, William T. **Psychologic Foundations of Education.** 1899.

Harris, William T. **Report of the Committee of Fifteen on the Elementary School.** 1895.

Harveson, Mae Elizabeth. **Catharine Esther Beecher: Pioneer Educator.** 1932.

Jackson, George Leroy. **The Development of School Support in Colonial Massachusetts.** 1909.

Kandel, I. L., editor. **Twenty-five Years of American Education.** 1924.

Kemp, William Webb. **The Support of Schools in Colonial New York by the Society for the Propagation of the Gospel in Foreign Parts.** 1913.

Kilpatrick, William Heard. **The Dutch Schools of New Netherland and Colonial New York.** 1912.

Kilpatrick, William Heard. **The Educational Frontier.** 1933.

Knight, Edgar Wallace. **The Influence of Reconstruction on Education in the South.** 1913.

Le Duc, Thomas. **Piety and Intellect at Amherst College, 1865-1912.** 1946.

Maclean, John. **History of the College of New Jersey from Its Origin in 1746 to the Commencement of 1854.** 1877.

Maddox, William Arthur. **The Free School Idea in Virginia before the Civil War.** 1918.

Mann, Horace. **Lectures on Education.** 1855.

McCadden, Joseph J. **Education in Pennsylvania, 1801-1835, and Its Debt to Roberts Vaux.** 1855.

McCallum, James Dow. **Eleazar Wheelock.** 1939.

McCuskey, Dorothy. **Bronson Alcott, Teacher.** 1940.

Meiklejohn, Alexander. **The Liberal College.** 1920.

Miller, Edward Alanson. **The History of Educational Legislation in Ohio from 1803 to 1850.** 1918.

Miller, George Frederick. **The Academy System of the State of New York.** 1922.

Monroe, Will S. **History of the Pestalozzian Movement in the United States.** 1907.

Mosely Education Commission. **Reports of the Mosely Education Commission to the United States of America October-December, 1903.** 1904.

Mowry, William A. **Recollections of a New England Educator.** 1908.

Mulhern, James. **A History of Secondary Education in Pennsylvania.** 1933.

National Herbart Society. **National Herbart Society Yearbooks 1-5, 1895-1899.** 1895-1899.

Nearing, Scott. **The New Education: A Review of Progressive Educational Movements of the Day.** 1915.

Neef, Joseph. **Sketches of a Plan and Method of Education.** 1808.

Nock, Albert Jay. **The Theory of Education in the United States.** 1932.

Norton, A. O., editor. **The First State Normal School in America: The Journals of Cyrus Pierce and Mary Swift.** 1926.

Oviatt, Edwin. **The Beginnings of Yale, 1701-1726.** 1916.

Packard, Frederic Adolphus. **The Daily Public School in the United States.** 1866.

Page, David P. **Theory and Practice of Teaching.** 1848.

Parker, Francis W. **Talks on Pedagogics: An Outline of the Theory of Concentration.** 1894.

Peabody, Elizabeth Palmer. **Record of a School.** 1835.

Porter, Noah. **The American Colleges and the American Public.** 1870.

Reigart, John Franklin. **The Lancasterian System of Instruction in the Schools of New York City.** 1916.

Reilly, Daniel F. **The School Controversy (1891-1893).** 1943.

Rice, Dr. J. M. **The Public-School System of the United States.** 1893.

Rice, Dr. J. M. **Scientific Management in Education.** 1912.

Ross, Early D. **Democracy's College: The Land-Grant Movement in the Formative Stage.** 1942.

Rugg, Harold, et al. **Curriculum-Making: Past and Present.** 1926.

Rugg, Harold, et al. **The Foundations of Curriculum-Making.** 1926.

Rugg, Harold and Shumaker, Ann. **The Child-Centered School.** 1928.

Seybolt, Robert Francis. **Apprenticeship and Apprenticeship Education in Colonial New England and New York.** 1917.

Seybolt, Robert Francis. **The Private Schools of Colonial Boston.** 1935.

Seybolt, Robert Francis. **The Public Schools of Colonial Boston.** 1935.

Sheldon, Henry D. **Student Life and Customs.** 1901.

Sherrill, Lewis Joseph. **Presbyterian Parochial Schools, 1846-1870.** 1932 .

Siljestrom, P. A. **Educational Institutions of the United States.** 1853.

Small, Walter Herbert. **Early New England Schools.** 1914.

Soltes, Mordecai. **The Yiddish Press: An Americanizing Agency.** 1925.

Stewart, George, Jr. **A History of Religious Education in Connecticut to the Middle of the Nineteenth Century.** 1924.

Storr, Richard J. **The Beginnings of Graduate Education in America.** 1953.

Stout, John Elbert. **The Development of High-School Curricula in the North Central States from 1860 to 1918.** 1921.

Suzzallo, Henry. **The Rise of Local School Supervision in Massachusetts.** 1906.

Swett, John. **Public Education in California.** 1911.

Tappan, Henry P. **University Education.** 1851.

Taylor, Howard Cromwell. **The Educational Significance of the Early Federal Land Ordinances.** 1921.

Taylor, J. Orville. **The District School.** 1834.

Tewksbury, Donald G. **The Founding of American Colleges and Universities before the Civil War.** 1932.

Thorndike, Edward L. **Educational Psychology.** 1913-1914.

True, Alfred Charles. **A History of Agricultural Education in the United States, 1785-1925.** 1929.

True, Alfred Charles. **A History of Agricultural Extension Work in the United States, 1785-1923.** 1928.

Updegraff, Harlan. **The Origin of the Moving School in Massachusetts.** 1908.

Wayland, Francis. **Thoughts on the Present Collegiate System in the United States.** 1842.

Weber, Samuel Edwin. **The Charity School Movement in Colonial Pennsylvania.** 1905.

Wells, Guy Fred. **Parish Education in Colonial Virginia.** 1923.

Wickersham, J. P. **The History of Education in Pennsylvania.** 1885.

Woodward, Calvin M. **The Manual Training School.** 1887.

Woody, Thomas. **Early Quaker Education in Pennsylvania.** 1920.

Woody, Thomas. **Quaker Education in the Colony and State of New Jersey.** 1923.

Wroth, Lawrence C. **An American Bookshelf, 1755.** 1934.

Series II

Adams, Evelyn C. **American Indian Education.** 1946.

Bailey, Joseph Cannon. **Seaman A. Knapp: Schoolmaster of American Agriculture.** 1945.

Beecher, Catharine and Harriet Beecher Stowe. **The American Woman's Home.** 1869.

Benezet, Louis T. **General Education in the Progressive College.** 1943.

Boas, Louise Schutz. **Woman's Education Begins.** 1935.

Bobbitt, Franklin. **The Curriculum.** 1918.

Bode, Boyd H. **Progressive Education at the Crossroads.** 1938.

Bourne, William Oland. **History of the Public School Society of the City of New York.** 1870.

Bronson, Walter C. **The History of Brown University, 1764-1914.** 1914.

Burstall, Sara A. **The Education of Girls in the United States.** 1894.

Butts, R. Freeman. **The College Charts Its Course.** 1939.

Caldwell, Otis W. and Stuart A. Courtis. **Then & Now in Education, 1845-1923.** 1923.

Calverton, V. F. & Samuel D. Schmalhausen, editors. **The New Generation: The Intimate Problems of Modern Parents and Children.** 1930.

Charters, W. W. **Curriculum Construction.** 1923.

Childs, John L. **Education and Morals.** 1950.

Childs, John L. Education and the Philosophy of Experimentalism. 1931.
Clapp, Elsie Ripley. Community Schools in Action. 1939.
Counts, George S. The American Road to Culture: A Social Interpretation of Education in the United States. 1930.
Counts, George S. School and Society in Chicago. 1928.
Finegan, Thomas E. Free Schools. 1921.
Fletcher, Robert Samuel. A History of Oberlin College. 1943.
Grattan, C. Hartley. In Quest of Knowledge: A Historical Perspective on Adult Education. 1955.
Hartman, Gertrude & Ann Shumaker, editors. Creative Expression. 1932.
Kandel, I. L. The Cult of Uncertainty. 1943.
Kandel, I. L. Examinations and Their Substitutes in the United States. 1936.
Kilpatrick, William Heard. Education for a Changing Civilization. 1926.
Kilpatrick, William Heard. Foundations of Method. 1925.
Kilpatrick, William Heard. The Montessori System Examined. 1914.
Lang, Ossian H., editor. Educational Creeds of the Nineteenth Century. 1898.
Learned, William S. The Quality of the Educational Process in the United States and in Europe. 1927.
Meiklejohn, Alexander. The Experimental College. 1932.
Middlekauff, Robert. Ancients and Axioms: Secondary Education in Eighteenth-Century New England. 1963.
Norwood, William Frederick. Medical Education in the United States Before the Civil War. 1944.
Parsons, Elsie W. Clews. Educational Legislation and Administration of the Colonial Governments. 1899.
Perry, Charles M. Henry Philip Tappan: Philosopher and University President. 1933.
Pierce, Bessie Louise. Civic Attitudes in American School Textbooks. 1930.
Rice, Edwin Wilbur. The Sunday-School Movement (1780-1917) and the American Sunday-School Union (1817-1917). 1917.
Robinson, James Harvey. The Humanizing of Knowledge. 1924.
Ryan, W. Carson. Studies in Early Graduate Education. 1939.
Seybolt, Robert Francis. The Evening School in Colonial America. 1925.
Seybolt, Robert Francis. Source Studies in American Colonial Education. 1925.
Todd, Lewis Paul. Wartime Relations of the Federal Government and the Public Schools, 1917-1918. 1945.
Vandewalker, Nina C. The Kindergarten in American Education. 1908.
Ward, Florence Elizabeth. The Montessori Method and the American School. 1913.
West, Andrew Fleming. Short Papers on American Liberal Education. 1907.
Wright, Marion M. Thompson. The Education of Negroes in New Jersey. 1941.

Supplement

The Social Frontier (Frontiers of Democracy). Vols. 1-10, 1934-1943.